SCANDALOUS!

SCANDALOUS!

Dark Times in the Life of Kiki Malachite

VANESSA MATEO

iUniverse, Inc.
Bloomington

SCANDALOUS!
Dark Times in the Life of Kiki Malachite

iUniverse books may be ordered through booksellers or by contacting:

iUniverse
1663 Liberty Drive
Bloomington, IN 47403
www.iuniverse.com
1-800-Authors (1-800-288-4677)

ISBN: 978-1-4759-2993-5 (sc)
ISBN: 978-1-4759-2994-2 (ebk)

Printed in the United States of America

iUniverse rev. date: 06/01/2012

CONTENTS

INTRODUCTION

My name is Kiki Malachite and I love men. I was born Marquivelian de Guinto in Manila, Philippines sometime in the late 1970s. In an attempt to 'Westernize' my name, I recently adopted the name "Kiki Malachite." After all, malachite is one of my favorite green gemstones. I can't reveal my true age or date of birth though. A true lady doesn't do that.

You may call me "Kei Kei" or "Po kei-kei." You may also call me "bitch", "slut" or "whore." I don't care. They are true anyway . . . if you *really* believe it. I love red lipstick, mile-long pearls, big bottles of Chanel 5 and red high heels. Yes, I suppose you can call me a girl of colorful character, but . . . I don't *work* the streets!

The streets are dangerous these days. I just love to stay in my dimly lit hotel room and accommodate my lovers. There is something sexy about a dark room—or the handsome faces in the dark for that matter. I feel like a captive, a sexual prisoner of some sort. And the handsome men are the demons and devils with their equally dark intentions. Oh, their big *horns* and even bigger libido; their blazing stares and burning desires! It boasts an ominous atmosphere, no doubt, but very exciting for some strange reason.

I just love being with married and involved men especially when they join me in my dark room. Ah yes, the shirt and tie; that undeniable fresh Zest scent with a hint of Old Spice the minute he lays down his body with his elbows up; and the soothing line "I love you baby" that I so love hearing constantly. It's a strange feeling of empowerment; but no commitments, of course. I'm only here for the fun and pleasure. I have learned my lesson from past experiences: you fall in love and sooner or later you'd feel like you've literally fallen and hit your head hard on the ground—because of the pain of betrayal. So, just love the body but not the heart.

That's the sad-but-true realization for me. Having relationships is a gamble. I win some and then I lose some. So, I just tend to have a "winner takes all" attitude most of the time.

Now let's go to the good stuff. Men are like Godiva candies—there's variety, they are a tongue teaser and I just can't get enough of them.

I love their smell, their taste and the way they please my senses.

I love the sexy things they whisper in my ear while they are romancing and ravaging my *aching* body. I could feel their soul that way; their very essence, which is to please and *release*.

I have some stories to tell, too, about my good, dark, bad and fun experiences in life. I believe these stories are worthy of telling. Whether or not they may be of interest to readers today because of their graphic sexual details, I think at some point, there will surface a group of cool people who are fairly open-minded to such facts, acts and revelations. I hope these scandalous excerpts from my private life would be good reading to them, especially in our world of today where wars and natural calamities are commonplace. I hope this book would serve as some form of temporary relief and diversion to them. I also hope my memoir would serve as some sort of a guideline to the different kinds of personal and sexual relationships, which sooner or later, those readers might find experiencing. As Dionne's boyfriend, Murray, from the 1995 hit movie *Clueless* once stated, "I'm keeping it real."

CHAPTER ONE

From Childhood to Chorizos

"Am I a girl or a boy?" was my initial question to myself the minute I became aware of my sexual orientation. It was more than thirty years ago. Although I was born male genetically, I have always *seen* my self as a girl. I enjoyed the company of girls in my neighborhood. Barbie dolls brightened my day and boys' basketball games—organized by my dad in our neighborhood—scared me to death. I would scream out "I don't want to play!" Naturally, it fell on deaf ears.

Surely, I am good at doing certain things, but I have reservations about using the word "good" when it comes to describing my self or another person. I mean, how good can you be? Nobody's perfect.

Now that I am in my thirties, I know I am definitely good in the bedroom. I say this because I love to *eat* men—their cocks, their *pinga*, *chorizos*, or whatever you call them—and I know for sure that I am very good at it. No, I am not talking about the movie *An American Werewolf in London*. Are you kidding me? I don't leave other people's husbands and boyfriends bleeding to death after I *eat* them, rather I leave them alive, with a heartbeat as fast as those NASCAR drivers, catching their breath and begging for more action!

Entice and excite. That's my mantra when it comes to seduction.

I will elaborate more as this chapter progresses.

Here's a brief summary, though, of my childhood years.

Growing up, I knew I was a good girl. I was obedient, respectful, courteous and sweet. I didn't have good grades in school though. Who cares! At a very young age, I wanted to live life by the day; take it as it is, and not live out the plans and dreams other people had for me. I believe the second I came out of this world, my first baby cries really meant "Don't fuck with me!"

I did enjoy playing with Barbie, Cabbage Patch and Strawberry Shortcake dolls, and enjoyed the company of girls my age. Nothing out of the ordinary, I guess. From time to time, I had crushes, too. But affairs and relationships with boys won't spring up until my 20s.

Nowadays, I enjoy playing with the big boys and their toys; with the real Kens as well as the Kents and Kyles out there. I believe my free-spirited nature from such a young age definitely contributed to my open-mindedness today, and also to my being unconventional.

My grade school years were okay. I just couldn't wait to get done with it. I was young and bored. Aside from the momentary excitement some cartoon shows like *The Smurfs, He-Man, She-Ra* and *Rainbow Brite* brought, my younger years were pretty much uneventful. But one thing's for sure in which I am totally proud about: I had a wonderful childhood. I thank my parents, grand-parents and other concerned relations for that. No bullies, no molesters, no old perverts. No, *no* shit of that kind!

I also think my family name served as a deterrent to would-be bullies and jerks. People around me knew which family I came from. My clan was well-known and well respected in that part of Manila. Half of the men in my clan were police officers. In plain and simple terms, we were *untouchable*.

I also enjoyed playing with the caterpillars lurking in my grandmother's garden. I remember getting very excited whenever I see a millipede (which was rare). That was quite a treat for me.

Another childhood recollection I have relates to my paternal great-great grandmother (who was over 100 years old at the time), Choleng, sitting on her *tumba tumba* (Tagalog term for "rocking chair"), tapping her withered hands on the chair's arm rest in a peculiar fashion but with seemingly perfect rhythm and timing. It gave me the impression that her life clock was ticking its way to the end. This was back in 1983. Within a few months, she was dead.

I also remember writing a promissory note of some sort to my cousins in Manila; that when I become successful and made a lot of money, I would send them dollars. Done that! I even sent their parents and a whole bunch of relatives some money. But, that's that. Let's go back to the main topic—my uneventful childhood.

Well, to make the long story short, there was not a lot of stories to be shared about my childhood, except when my father beat my boy ass hard with a leather belt when he found out I had my first manicure and pedicure; or remembering those '80s dance hits such as "Body Dancer", "Swiss Boy", "Never Mind Her" and "Rhythm of the Night" becoming radio favorites in the Philippines. And who could forget the sentimental ballads "If You're Not Here" and "Please be Good to Me" by Menudo? Wow. Now, I guess I'm *talking*.

I also remember having a couple of distant relatives as teachers in my grade school years and the discrimination I experienced from them just because my first cousin, Ramon, who was also my fellow classmate, had fair skin and looked *mestizo*. They would pick on me from time to time. Ironically, those two former teachers were first cousins themselves.

In the Philippines, you are automatically judged by the shade of your complexion; the lighter the better and more "ideal"; the darker, the less appealing. Ingrained in the minds of some Filipinos there is the colonial mentality exemplified by the Spaniards many centuries ago: fair complexion and aquiline noses were the standard beauty hallmarks of the day; and dark skinned, short and flat-nosed people were called *indios*, almost considered sub humans.

But, of course, I did not let the minor atrocities concocted by my former teachers affect me. "After all," I told myself, "Miss Capong had darker skin than me. She should be the one tormenting herself, and her cousin takes food from Hazel's (one of my classmates) lunch box. Gross!"

At any rate, I did my homework and submitted my school projects and in the end, received my grade school diploma. That was it.

Also during the 1980s, I enjoyed playing Pac Man and Space Invaders on Atari and Super Mario Bros and The Legend of Zelda on Nintendo.

In the early '90s, I also attended high school in Manila. Those were fun times: high school crushes, cutting classes and cute asses.

I remember my fervent admiration towards a cute guy named Edson. I think that was the major reason why I went to class; not so much for perfect attendance and good grades. Seeing him every day was a good thing. In 1995, one year after migrating to the US, I sent him a greeting card, telling him how I was so secretively fond of him during our high school years. He used to live along a street in Caloocan City called Libis Nadurata.

A couple of my friends and I would cut classes, too, occasionally. At one point, our Home Economics teacher—Miss Dicho—caught us hanging around at a nearby cafeteria during school hours. As we attempted to walk away, the hawk-eyed teacher caught and reprimanded us, saying "Hey, hey, hey! Where do you think you guys are going?"

I also liked participating in those so-called 'Speech Choir' contests wherein your entire class would do a monologue type of speech and compete with other students from other classes. I also remember hanging out with friends at my classmate Paquita Sevilla's three-story house near Hermosa Street and lip-synching Lisa Lisa and the Cult Jam's "Lost in Emotion" while toying with their Yamaha keyboard. I also relish the times when my good friend, Robbie, would invite me and other friends to his house in Caloocan City and watch adult films from which, on one occasion, provoked some of the guys to do a "gang rape scene"; my other gay friend, Juvie, being the unfortunate "victim". The brusque boys kicked us out of the TV room and god only knows what they did to Juvie. Crazy! Lastly, I think the Boys Locker Room or "Prosti House" (a term me and my two other gay friends coined), and the crazy stuff we did there, are the most memorable. In that locker room, me and my gay friends would flirt and mingle with the straight guys while changing into our P.E. uniform, and eventually would hide under its stairs when the time comes for us to join the other boys to play basketball for which we were individually graded. I remember making an unprecedented request to my P.E. teacher: that I'd prefer to be graded while playing with the girls' team instead of the boys'. Luckily for me, he acquiesced.

Also, sometime in 1992, I was one of the three St. Joseph High students who represented our school at the District Spelling Bee Contest. We ended up in second place. In the same year, I saw *Bram Stoker's Dracula* and *Chaplin* with some of my classmates and friends. Keanu Reeves became an instant Hollywood crush.

I also recall, with great fondness and appreciation, the visits my other friends, Orante and Itzel, made months before I flew to the United States. This was in early 1994, one year after our high school graduation. We were already in our own separate ways—college bound and contemplating adult life—but it was nice to see them from time to time and catch up on things. Before Orante leaves, we'd do a duet of the song "Let Me Be Your Wings" from *Thumbelina*.

Deep inside me, I knew those final meetings meant "Good-bye."

In September 1994, it was time for my family to move to the US. I'll never forget the expression on my cousin's face—Lynna—as I hopped out of the family van upon arriving at the airport: devoid of life and hope. It was like she wanted to tell me "Take me with you" or "Please don't go." I never knew the meaning of the word "forlorn"—in the most realistic sense—until after that scene. Her parents were on the brink of separation during that time and how I wish I stayed a little longer to offer her some consolation and emotional support.

Fast forward: California life in the fall season of 1994. My father advised that I should take two years of high school to earn a High School Diploma. I had to obey, much to my chagrin.

Life was completely different. I definitely felt the pressure; the pressure to earn good grades and look attractive.

I didn't succumb to the 'looking good' part, thankfully. I kept my head straight and focused on my studies instead of focusing on who's the coolest student around. I wanted to make my parents proud. I needed a high school Diploma, for crying out loud! We all know that having a High School Diploma here in the US is like having a Free Pass to major events: opportunities and more opportunities!

Soon enough though, I became distracted by the events that were taking place in pop culture. The Cranberries' "Zombie" and Madonna's "Secret" hit the charts; not to forget Hole's "Doll Parts" and Soundgarden's "Black Hole Sun". The King of Pop, Michael Jackson, marries The King's daughter, Lisa Marie Presley. CNN's *Style with Elsa Klensch* was still in *style* back then.

In my high school, Bill Hanz was an angelic figure back then. Oh, you should've seen how my jaw dropped when he passed by my Sociology classroom back in 1995. He was literally a vision in white—flawless, alabaster complexion and reddish cheeks. It was the very first time I saw him, and fifteen years later, his beautiful face still haunts me. Unforgettable!

Yes, there were times when I felt envious of some Mountain Range High girls with slutty tendencies like Tonette, Lassie and Daniella, but I did *not* want to be a slut like them yet. I wanted to keep my *hole* fresh, tight and smelling good for the right man, *or* men for that matter.

By 1996, I am a high school grad—and still a virgin—and by the following year I have completely transformed myself from looking male into a female transgender person or T-girl. I also found myself working as a receptionist for a now-defunct small telecommunications company in Fremont, CA.

I got fired though. I got fired after a year of service because instead of doing customer service duties, I got caught *servicing* the handsome supervisor, Tim Spears. I blew it! No. I *blew* him!

The big boss, and I mean, she was *really* big (like a Whirlpool washer), Miss Verlaz, unfortunately caught me and Tim in the act one chilly February morning in 1999. Apparently, she had been trying to get in at her office but the door was locked. She had to ask another supervisor to forcibly open the door.

Totally unaware of the dreadful scene that was about to unfold, the handsome supervisor and I locked ourselves in to do the nasty. We assumed Miss V won't show up to work until 10 that morning. She normally comes in around 8 on weekdays except Fridays (when she would come in late; "manager special" as I labeled those Fridays with contempt). I loathe company time cheaters and abusers. They are no different than thieves and burglars. Scum of the earth!

So, Miss V caught me sitting on the male supervisor's lap with my top off and making out with the latter. I could clearly remember her facial expression, comparable to that of the evil stepmother of Cinderella the minute she found out the latter had kept the other pair of glass slippers after all. Miss V turned even whiter than white; so white that I thought she'd drop dead on the spot from a heart attack.

She survived though, but not my job.

From March to May 1999, I had odd jobs. I had to put up with it. I carried on. Deep inside me, I still knew I was a good girl. Only the circumstances were bad, but not me.

In retrospect, the first twenty-two years of my life had been normal and somewhat fun. Maybe I was a good girl after all. By the summer of 1999, I became bored with the mediocre trappings of suburban life: a minimum-wage-paying part-time job at a clothing store, a part-time babysitting job and basically having no clear directions in life.

So, by the fall season in 1999, I embarked on an adventure . . . with men. I was not the pretty type. I just knew I was attractive and had an enormous amount of sex appeal. I had dark, long hair, big tits (thanks to Avon, So-En and Mondragon bras and undergarments), soft, brown skin and legs to die for. I remember my first trip to this Downtown Mountain View bar that summer. My girl friend, Lulu, asked the bartender what my most attractive physical trait was. John the Bartender just replied, "Her eyes."

So, the eyes have it. John was right. His words were prophetic. In the ensuing years, my lovers would constantly comment on how sexy and seductive my eyes are especially while I am looking up to them as I give them pleasure. "Damn, girl! Your eyes look like Liv Tyler's when you look at me like that!" a one-time lover from Hayward, CA once commented.

I suppose during those times I was not the boring girl anymore—the "At Seventeen" type of girl Janis Ian used to sing about. I am now the girl with lots of sex appeal and lots of men kneeling before her; a girl with a big heart and an even bigger tongue.

My big fat tongue could do wonders. I have been told once by an ex-lover that it cured his depression.

Andrew, my handsome and rich lover since 2006 once asked me if his butt was big. "Big, beefy and sexy!" was my excited response. I had a counter question: "Is my tongue big?"

"Very! It feels so damn good, too!" Andrew replied.

Hilarious! Why was I even asking that question? Every time I look in the mirror and stick my tongue out, all I could say afterwards is "Thank you, Lord, for this big, fat tongue."

Men just love my big, fat tongue all over them. Oh yes, *the* tongue.

I wouldn't trade it for the Crown of England, Wall Street or the gold bars locked inside the fabled vaults of those Swiss banks. Never! I consider it a priceless treasure—even an investment—just like my fabulous jewelry collection. This big, fat tongue is irreplaceable!

It's an investment for life.

CHAPTER TWO

Beautiful Men

I love beautiful things and beautiful men. Living a happy, contented life is good, but seeing beautiful men and pretty boys every day is a bonus. To me, it's one of the things that make life worthy of living. I *have* to see beauty. I have to feel and *breathe* it. I am thirsty for it. And in men, I find it.

Men are considered the "upper" sex; the more powerful gender. Amen to that. I love men. I worship men. I adore men. They are like water to me; without them, survival would be tough for me. I can't imagine myself having no sexy and strong stud lying next to me, satiating my carnal cravings. I might as well join Annie and the orphans in singing "It's The Hard Knock Life" if that ever happens.

"It's a man's world," we often hear. Some might disagree. Who cares? One thing I am sure of—men *rule* my world.

Adam was God's first human creation: father of all fathers. To Adam, I am very thankful.

His 21st century descendants whom I've had the privilege of meeting and *knowing* are some of the best. The men in my life are not only good, but they are also some of the most beautiful: Chris, Russ, Neil, and a bunch more. *Hallelujah!*, shouts this happy whore.

I also would like to pay homage to the beautiful men who have graced this planet since time immemorial.

During the period of Antiquity, the world witnessed the birth and rise of beautiful men like Paris, Adonis, and Narcissus. Their inherent beauty had been glorified through thousands of books and poems written, and served as an inspiration to many artists and painters through the ages.

These days, the male beauty is still considered a high commodity. Just like in books, paintings and sculptures where a handsome man is depicted, beauty can still be purchased. Lustful old men and women have no issues when it comes to paying for the "private" services of a handsome male escort; modeling agencies pay top-dollar for the best male faces and bodies to appear on the runway; and recruiters for potential adult magazine models woo their subjects with a substantial amount of money.

In short, male beauty is power, and to have power means you could accumulate money and riches easily. When you're beautiful, you're in control. Recruiters and agents dance to your music, even if they sometimes appear reluctant to your requests and demands (like what we see in some reality shows). Rest assured that by the end of the day, they are sure to kiss your ass anyway.

Luckily for me, I don't have to pay a single penny to have a beautiful man beside me.

It's all about making the right choices at the right time. Thankfully, the goddess of love and beauty, Venus, has been very kind to me. She makes sure I have plenty of beautiful *things* to go around with. I have met and *experienced* almost every type of man in existence: eighteen and nineteen year-old studs, twenty-something heartthrobs, handsome single fathers, divorced daddies and willing widowers. They were all beautiful.

Age didn't matter to me at all nor did their profession. There were men in uniform; there were doctors, software engineers, bank managers, architects, foremen, construction workers, lawyers, waiters and college students. There were the unemployed, too. I didn't really care about what they do. I just cared about how they'd *do* me. As long as they're beautiful and are open to kinky things with me in the bedroom, they can *hop* in my wagon and on my wagging tongue anytime.

In the entertainment industry, whether or not it's in the form of reality shows, the movies or adult films, male beauty is a staple. Some notable actors and celebrities I adore include Jon Hamm, Paul Walker, Bradley Cooper, Chris Hemsworth, Ethan Hawke, Ryan Reynolds, Josh Harnett, Channing Tatum, Sean Faris, Cameron Mathison, Josh Lucas, Chris Evans, Michael Vartan, Chris Pine, Eric Dane, Sam Witwer, Kellan Lutz, Christopher Meloni, Ty Pennington, Evan Farmer, Jason Cameron, Anderson Cooper, Thomas Roberts, Mike Rowe, TJ Cummings, Jack Venice, Ramon Nomar, Marc Dylan, Nick Sterling, Scott Styles, Zak Bagans, Jessie Pavelka, Bear Grylles and Dave Salmoni.

I also have a soft spot for the hard-bodied men of sports. They include Alex Smith, Aaron Rodgers, Tim Tebow, Drew Brees, Tom Brady, Mark Mulder, Cliff Lee, Cole Hamels, David Lee, Kevin Love, Jason Kidd, Andre Agassi, Tyler Hansbrough, John Cena, Randy Orton, AJ Styles, Wade Barrett, Ted DiBiase Jr. and believe it or not, Tampa Bay Buccaneers head coach himself, Jon Gruden. I believe Gruden's foul mouth on the football field is perfect for my S&M sessions.

But what are really the factors that constitute male beauty? Good genes and good skin are some of them, for sure.

I believe sex appeal is also an important factor. Take Mike Rowe as an example. In his TV series, *Dirty Jobs*, he portrays the character of a rough and rugged mature man ready to conquer grease, stench and grime. Now, that's macho. But then again, Rowe doesn't have the so-called 'pretty' face. Still, I am attracted to him, as well as a good number of gay men out there. Simply put, beauty is also in the form of projection; it's not just a profitable possession.

I've always felt a special attraction towards construction men in filthy white T-shirts and blue jeans. I always get this erotic visual of how their bodies would look like with no clothes on. Also, I fantasize about pleasing them with just their construction boots and hard hat on. It might sound kinky, but to me, a man does not need to be in an Armani suit to make the cut . . . and to make my tongue wag. For all I care, he could just be in a white wife-beater and a pair of Levi's, and still look delectable.

I have to admit, I have the hots for Mike Rowe. His athletic physique, deep voice and come-see-me-tonight blue eyes are enough to ignite my inner fire. Rowe, although not the handsomest face on TV, is one of the most beautiful men around in my opinion. Again, it's what he projects that makes him very attractive.

Other TV personalities I adore who aren't afraid to get sweaty and dirty in front of the camera are Evan Farmer, Ty Pennington and Jason Cameron.

Every drop of sweat from their bodies is like a drop of gold. They get paid *to* sweat. Amazing! If those drops of sweat literally turned into gold nuggets and were to be sold, Cash 4 Gold would go bankrupt!

A major fantasy of mine would be to have these three gorgeous guys work on my house. But I doubt *if* there will be any serious work done though.

Male beauty should not be limited to having perfect looks alone. I believe being beautiful is also representative of certain physical characteristics such as an imperfect nose, a cleft lip scar, a unique tattoo, or some facial scar. Prominent celebrities with such imperfections include Chad Michael Murray, Joachim Phoenix and Seal. I may not be attracted to the last two but surely they are admired by millions.

"Beauty is in the eye of the beholder," the old adage goes. People have different standards and perceptions when it comes to the subject of what's beautiful. In my case, I find myself easily attracted to good-looking men in their mid 30s and early 40s. The lines on their forehead represent maturity and knowledge. Their straight-back posture suggests confidence. The slightly loosened tie bemoans the easy-go-lucky attitude, and their "I've-experienced-it-all" aura says "I can do you, too." It's very sexy.

What's more exciting and sexy is when I start to loosen up the tie of one of my lovers belonging to that age group while kneeling down, and proceed to *go down* on him `*a la* Julia Roberts in *Pretty Woman*. But then again I believe I give a better blow job than Roberts' character in that movie. Her style is comparable to that of "small fry" teenage girls and dormitory sluts: terribly amateurish.

Caucasian men with dark hair and blue, green or hazel eyes turn me on a great deal. Think of Cameron Mathison, *Ghost Adventures* star Zak Bagans and *The Insider* co-anchor Thomas Roberts. How I'd love to have a foursome with these gorgeous men.

A friend of mine once commented, "You're into the Freddie Prinze Jr. type." He was absolutely right.

San Francisco 49ers quarterback, Alex Smith, is another eye-candy. His tapered eyebrows somehow inexplicably intrigue and captivate me. Why, I don't know. Arguably, his eyes are the sexiest and most beautiful I have seen in a quarterback. Not to mention the body and butt. Now, that's what I call a real bonus! I could really care less for those Season Tickets. I only care about his good looking jock ass for the entire season!

Mad Men star Jon Hamm is another TV treat. Nothing is more perfect than a lazy Thursday night at home with me undraping Don Draper with my eyes.

Jon or Don, it doesn't matter to me; both personas are beautiful in my eyes.

There is also a significant reason behind my attraction to Jon Hamm: he has a striking resemblance to one of my former lovers whom I dated for four long years. A face like that is simply hard to forget.

When you've had beauty dominating your body and soul for such a long time, how could you forget?

I also find blonds with beefy, muscular bodies and "baby" faces very attractive. Adult film star TJ Cummings, *DietTribe* host Jessie Pavelka, and Discovery Channel's Dave Salmoni are on top of my list. They are *the* vanilla cupcakes that I'd love to lick from start to finish. I can't get enough of them.

Sex god TJ Cummings has the best ass I've seen in a man from the porn world; bar none. He looks so *delicious*! I can never recall the many times I've daydreamed and fantasized about him. His bubble butt is as pretty as his face. It's hard to decide which of the two I like best.

Of course, this book won't go unread without me paying homage to the lovers I have with the sexiest and roundest bubble butts one could ever imagine messing around with. If Europe has its *Almanach de Gotha*, conversely, I have my own *Almanach de Booty*. Topping my list are Nate, Chris, Mark, John, Andrew and Neil. Oh yes Scarlett O'Hara, like you, I'll never go hungry again!

My world will stop revolving and life will be irreparably boring without beautiful men in my surroundings. Beautiful men are my happiness and satisfaction. Well, of course, my gold and diamonds, too.

Hey, I wouldn't mind rubbing the *bats* of Cliff Lee and Cole Hamels at the same time! But I want them both bending over on my loveseat. Oh, my dark and dirty fantasies!

CHAPTER THREE

Playing with Kiki

"Wait around here for a couple of minutes before you knock okay?" was Mike's strict instruction before he went inside the dark and dirty men's restroom at the Chevron gas station along McKee and Capitol in San Jose. He wanted me to give him a blow job inside.

A *runaway slut* who likes to give head; yes, that's how I was to some of these strangers—the "Bad Boys" in the early years of my being a wild T-girl.

2000 was the year I started reveling in my newfound freedom, the freedom to become a full-time slut.

You know the saying 'Experience is everything'? Well, I wanted to experience *every* thing. I was very excited and always looked forward to experiencing new things and having kinky sexual encounters with married or *involved* men. Once again, I became slave to my darkest desires and the faces in the dark who were willing to fulfill them.

I was young and wild. I was constantly ready for some action. I didn't care much as to with who I'm going to do *it* with. To me, the main goal was to be with men so I could feel appreciated.

As expected, the men took advantage of my naivety and passiveness. In me, they found a living and breathing fuck doll and blow job machine. Some offered monetary compensation, some insisted on getting freebies.

Either way, I obliged.

Mike was an average-looking Joe in his early forties who worked for a hi-tech company in San Jose. He would pick me up some afternoons during the week in his lifted old Chevy Suburban and we'd park at some discreet location in the area. There, he would get his pleasure from my skilled and willing mouth. He was satisfied, but I was not. At one point, we even did it up in Mount Hamilton.

We met close to a dozen times. By the latter part of 2000, the sexual romps ended. I was getting tired of the same old guy, and the same old scene. I was craving for my *own* satisfaction, and when I came to the realization that Mike was not willing to give it to me, I turned my back on him and dropped him like a piece of trash.

You treat me like garbage, the same thing will happen to you.

But sometimes the garbage you throw has a strange way of coming back to you. Twice I saw him driving along the 880 freeway in Fremont, CA and along Mathilda Avenue in Sunnyvale; with a female passenger. I assumed it was his wife or girlfriend.

Another cheapskate who would constantly chase me for my oral skills was this middle-aged, fat white guy from Santa Cruz, CA. Bill was a Corvette-driving pervert who even performed S&M scenes with me on one occasion.

I met Bill through Yahoo! Personals in mid-2000. In his profile, he claimed he was looking for a t-girl to date and take out to nice dinners, blah, blah, blah. I became excited over the idea so I replied.

The thought of being finally treated like a real lady—with the dinner and movie treats—was very appealing to me. It was the kind of experience I was looking for. I thought Bill was the answer to my prayers.

Things were to turn appalling instead. It turned out I would be *kneeling* not to pray for blessings to come, but to do something else rather.

Bill didn't even give me the courtesy of bringing me to a hotel. This Corvette-riding cheapo even came by my apartment to do his nasty business. Another uncomfortable scene was when he forced me to do the *nasty* in the backseat of my beat up Pinto. It was deplorable.

Finally, in early 2001, I decided to throw this dirty old pig back in the corral; for good. I never saw him again after that.

Steve Mael was a 30-something Latin guy with shaved head and a penchant for hot tub hook-ups. He was very good-looking, but was not the best suited to give girls like myself better treatment.

All he wanted was to get a good blow job. He would rent us a room at the Grand Central Spas in San Jose. We'd come in, do our nasty business and exit the door as if we didn't know each other. No hugs, no "Good-bye."

It was that bad and alienating. Every time I hopped in my car after such encounter, I would pause and ask myself if it's really worth it.

All these degrading scenes continued until the middle part of 2001. I would've looked at it differently had I gotten my pleasure and satisfaction. The problem was that they were all selfish.

In June of that year, I finally met someone who somehow gave me better treatment and showed some appreciation: JC. You will hear more about him later.

The influx of bad boys in the early years of my "naughty T-girl years" did not only involve Mike, Bill and Steve. Regardless, I am now putting these dark and dehumanizing experiences behind me. It's high time that I recognize and thank the good guys and the gentlemen I've met.

CHAPTER FOUR

Gentlemen Prefer Browns

After the bad dates I had in the early years of my being a wild T-girl, fate had finally brought me good things and good men. I believe in good karma: when someone takes advantage of you, sooner or later, opportunities of an advantageous nature will arrive at your doorstep.

During those times that I had been used, I knew very well all I wanted in return was a little respect and better treatment. I wasn't expecting much. Still, the bad men I met before deprived me of those little things. Now, I've turned the tables around. I'd like to honor and thank these few handsome gentlemen for making me believe that beauty is not just on the outside, it is also skin deep; and that beautiful things could still come my way.

In my private journals, I've acknowledged these two great men—Jim and Michael—and the respect and love they've bestowed on me. For some reason, I've unintentionally omitted the names of several other individuals who are also worthy of an honorable mention.

Jeff Bartel was a thirty-five year-old computer engineer from San Jose whom I met through Craigslist in the spring of 2005. He was, by far, the nicest man—and one of the most beautiful. In plain and simple terms, he "swept me off my feet."

The numerous lunch and dinner dates we had are an attestation that he had good intentions. When other men would suggest that we proceed to the bedroom or hotel room on the first date, Jeff suggested that we head to my favorite restaurant instead. He wanted to know *me* first, not my bedroom capabilities.

There were hot, kinky sex, of course, but those came in later. When that finally happened, Jeff gave it to me with an option: he could be rough or romantic, depending on how I felt at the moment. He respected my limits and was also open to granting me my special "kinky wishes". I savor and treasure all the memories I have of him.

Jeff took me out lunching at several restaurants within Santa Clara County. He was *that* confident with me. He was never embarrassed to be seen in public with me: a wild T-girl in denim mini skirts, high heels and shoulder-baring tops. I really admire and thank him for that.

Whenever he'd come visit me at my hotel room, he was the epitome of a true gentleman: with a bouquet of flowers at hand or a box of chocolates. As a matter of fact, I've preserved some of the roses he gave me. Although they are now dry and brittle, they serve as a constant reminder of the respect and appreciation Jeff had shown me.

For my 28th birthday in May of 2005, Jeff gave me a gorgeous pair of animal print heels as a present. This only validated our special friendship more. At that point, I knew Jeff was one of those few people who are truly 'for keeps'.

Mark Kimmel is a thirty-seven year-old single father from Morgan Hill, California. We met through the popular website Craigslist in the summer of 2005, a few months after I met Jeff.

Mark is very good-looking and an avid fan of motorcycles. Dirt-biking is one of his favorite pastimes. He works for a hi-tech company in Redwood City, California.

I always have a great time with Mark. Occasionally, we would dine out at his favorite Mexican restaurant, El Torito. Mark is of mixed race: half white, half Mexican; hence, his passion for anything Latin.

Also, Mark and I would have our *private* time at a hotel in Fremont. We are both passionate and kinky lovers. The sex and pleasure Mark gives me is the 'icing to the cake' to our beautiful, drama-free relationship.

Like Jeff, Mark grants me my "kinky wishes" whenever I'd ask for it. There are some occasions when I'd ask him to wear thong underwear because his beefy behind looks so good in it. It's one of the things that turn me on greatly. We've also experimented with whip cream, honey and Hershey's syrup. Those were delightful and *delicious* times.

My relationship with Mark is non-committal. Because of his status as a separated single father, I don't expect anything more beyond a few hours of companionship and intimacy. I totally understand his situation. His son needs him more than I do, no doubt. But I'm very thankful and appreciative of the time and attention my handsome lover bestows on me whenever opportunity allows him.

Patrick Larson and I first met in the fall of 2000, and five years later—in August 2005—we rekindled our "casual" relationship. The 'second time around' proved more memorable and special. That Friday evening in August 2005, Pat drove me to the Black Angus restaurant in Milpitas in his sporty dark-green BMW Z3 convertible.

It was a very exciting time for me. All eyes on the 880 freeway were on me—considering my tall frame, therefore making me more visible—and my strawberry blond hair. I loved the attention.

Inside Black Angus, it was all about recalling the fun times we had when we first met, and of course, feasting on steak and other specialties.

Back at the nice Holiday Inn hotel room that Pat got us after dinner, it was all about Kiki's pleasure and satisfaction. Pat made sure my bedroom happiness was achieved.

A week after our Friday rendezvous, Pat invited me to his nice pad in San Rafael, California. San Rafael is a city in Marin County noted for its prominent and wealthy residents. Pat was no exception.

Upon my arrival that Saturday afternoon, Pat surprised me with three large boxes of perfumes, lotions, and lingerie from Victoria's Secret.

It was overwhelming. In my utter excitement, I immediately tried on a silky peach-colored negligee` and ultimately wore it for the remainder of the night.

Pat was obviously smitten. He enjoyed seeing me draped in very sexy undergarments. It turned him on a great deal.

What's an appreciative and happy girl to do? Give the generous gentleman a lap dance he won't forget. *Pat Jr.* became very *excited.*

Pat also prepared a sumptuous dinner for me later that evening. Unfortunately, I was so weak to rise from the bed. Pat had to eat his meal alone. I was so embarrassed. But Pat, being the natural gentleman that he was, totally understood everything.

We shared a sexually gratifying night together. I felt that my head was high up the ceiling as I climaxed.

What set Pat apart from Jeff and Mike was his assertiveness when it came to *having* his own pleasure. I did not mind that at all. He made clear he would be in total control of the entire scene.

I respected that just because he was obliging enough to give me what pleased me hours earlier. It's just fair that I grant him his own sexual wishes in the bedroom.

The following morning when I woke up, Pat brought me coffee and a box of chocolates. I remember telling myself 'God, I wish every morning of my life is like this!'

CHAPTER FIVE

Curiosity and the Cats

"I've never done this before . . . you're my first" is my favorite line from the many curious Georges and Johns and other straight cats whom I've met in the past seven years of my exciting wild T-girl life. It was comparable to a long-playing album. Ask me if I ever get tired of hearing it though and I'll give you a flat "No" for an answer. Why? Because I think, straight men are the sexiest, most delightful group of men in the world.

It's a fantasy-come-true for me, no doubt. When gay men would only dream of a friendly smile from the straight boy next door, for Kiki, it's a totally different scenario. The only *dreaming* I'd do would take place in the middle of the night, while in deep slumber and dreaming about the most erotic time I had hours earlier with a very good-looking straight man.

You'd think I wouldn't want to wake up? You'd be surprised. Of course, I do! I'd like to wake up and start a new day, with hopes that I'd have another exciting time with the much-desired straight guy on the block.

Contrary to popular myth that heterosexual men try to avoid gays and transsexuals, in my personal experiences, some of the best fun I've had occurred while in the company of the former. Maybe some straight men really do *not* want anything to do with some gays and transsexuals, but I am totally alien to that, unless, of course, I find myself in a redneck state with a lot of stupid, mean and ignorant people. Then, I have to be very careful!

But in reality, I never had a bad or boring time with a straight guy.

They are a joy to be with. I like hearing their views and opinions on many things; I like knowing what they truly feel about being with me using straight up questions `a la* Soledad O'Brien; and I appreciate their willingness to be open to the kinky, dirty things I desire in the bedroom. That's all that matters. With that, I am proud to say I love and adore a lot of straight men.

It's all about the good and positive experiences I've had with these men. It's what garners them my respect. Here are some of the adorable straight men whom I've had the pleasure of meeting and *eating* over the years.

Mark O'Connell

Mark is a forty year-old married guy from Castro Valley, California who works for a hi-tech company in nearby Pleasanton. Originally a "generous friend" or someone who gives me cash gift after my encounter with him, our relationship became more *personal* when he expressed his most sincere offer to become my lover; *or* one of my lovers. I suppose he was instantly smitten by my charm, beauty and booty.

I felt good, positive vibes from him, not to mention liking his physical attributes: a handsome face and a nice build. He reminds me Alec Baldwin. He is tall—with Irish good looks—and has that "businessman appeal". He especially looks good in a shirt and tie combo and a pair of black shoes and socks. Whenever he'd come to visit dressed that way, I couldn't help but drop down on my knees in an instant.

The sex is always great. Mark makes sure my needs are met. Before he reaches orgasmic stage, he'd see to it that I've already *released*. Yes, Mark is a gentleman even in bed! That's what makes him my number one favorite.

Kevin McCarthy

"I came to California with nothing when I was 19," my handsome friend Kevin once shared. "Now, I'm doing well and have a good family."

It's not just Kevin's success that I admire about him the most; it's also his determination to do good things, not just for himself, but for others as well.

Kevin is a fifty year-old divorce` from Sunol, California with two grown up children. He manages a thriving construction business.

Kevin and I met through the popular hodgepodge website Craigslist. I was bored one evening and decided to post an ad on its *Casual Encounter* section; just taking a chance if I'd get lucky. After meeting Kevin, I'm proud to say that I'm not just lucky, but fortunate as well.

Kevin is one of the nicest straight guys around. His age and maturity are an attestation to his broad and open mind when it comes to certain things. He is well past that still-getting-over-it stage when it comes to some of life's realities; one of which pertains to him having sexual romps with a transsexual like me.

Being with Kevin is a nurturing experience. Our dates are enveloped with lively conversation and the best wine. From Kevin, I learn a lot. He also inspires me to become a better person; to remain focused on my endeavors and to work harder in reaching my goals.

Kevin also has a generous heart. Upon returning from Hawaii in early 2007, Kevin handed me a beautiful necklace made with natural Hawaiian stones and seashells as a souvenir present. He also included a box of chocolate-covered Macadamia nuts.

Kevin is as delicious as those Macadamia nuts in bed. At fifty, he knows a lot of things when it comes to pleasing his bedroom companion.

His age and maturity also turn me on in some kinky way. There are times when we'd role play: him as a naughty college professor and myself as a slutty college student.

I also have a penchant for having my lover wear construction gear or dress like a lawyer. I especially enjoy it whenever Kevin would show up in blue jeans and a dirty pair of construction boots with a hard hat on. Drill me, daddy!

Vincent Legiezzi

Vincent Legiezzi, or Vinny, is a forty five year-old businessman from San Diego, California. We met through the Yahoo! Personals dating site in late 2004. We've been communicating through online chat for a couple of months prior to that November 2004 meeting.

He was staying at the Hampton Inn not far from where I lived at the time of our meeting. When I arrived, there was a fine-looking gentleman waiting by the door, with a bottle of wine at hand. He was still in business attire: white shirt, a tie, a pair of black pants, black leather shoes and black socks. I was instantly turned on.

Vinny is the epitome of a classic Italian man: romantic, a true gentleman, and always in the *mood*.

The sexual tension was too high to ignore. We simply had to take care of "business". Vinny was my "Godfather" and I knew for sure I served him well that night. I believe I've kissed more than just his Signet ring during that encounter. Vinny was also considerate enough to give me what I needed. He pleased and satisfied me the way I wanted it.

I admit, having sex on the first date seems inappropriate, but I am a go-getter kind of person. Whenever I feel like doing or acquiring something, I'd go for it in an instant. *Carpe diem*! I always follow my instincts and make sure I don't repress myself. My sexual satisfaction and happiness are paramount.

Sex with Vinny is simply hard to resist. It has always been a pleasurable experience. I love every minute of it.

In our most recent telephone conversation, Vinny sounded as if he had been missing me terribly and having girlfriend problems. He uttered "I love you" some ten times. He also promised that the first thing he would do once he is given another opportunity to visit San Jose is to see me.

Talking about a major *drought* from Kiki's *loving!*

Jeffrey Broderick

My handsome, blue-eyed Canadian-American lover, Jeff Broderick of San Ramon, California, is a full time tow-truck driver. He is thirty-three years old, tall, single and all man. And he can *haul* my rear, the rear of my car that is, anytime! He drinks beer like water, smokes like a chimney and talks and fucks rough like a marine.

Those qualities turn me on big time, all the more making me feel very attracted to him.

Jeff responded to my Yahoo! Profile in late 2004. After weeks of online chat and regular e-mail exchange, we decided to meet. He invited me one December night to his home near Alcosta Boulevard in San Ramon.

Jeff had just broken up with his live-in girlfriend at the time. He said the latter was a "complete pain in the butt." The former companion apparently was lazy and had more drama in her than *All My Children*. Jeff, just like any other straight man, finds people with too much drama and emotional baggage abhorrent. He simply had to get rid of her.

Replacing the drama queen as Jeff's occasional evening companion was yours truly, sexy Kiki. Jeff and I always had a fun-filled, relaxing time together. Whenever I visit him, there is an ice cold bottle of Corona or Heineken that awaits me.

After some fifteen minutes of lively conversation regarding the new events and developments in our lives, we'd retire in his bedroom for a more intimate and pleasurable time. Jeff relishes the soothing massages I give him. He would always whisper "You have the magic touch" whenever I'd work on his stressed, aching back using my fantastic massaging skills.

After several minutes of continuous backrubs and oral pleasuring, Jeff would turn over and give me the wildest *ride*. He is *very* good. So good that he was one of the few lovers who made the black of my eye disappear from sheer pleasure.

'Damn, this is better than the Space Mountain ride!' I told myself once.

There were some occasions when Jeff would do justice towards my half-hour drive to his home. He would give me some cash gift as "gas money". I'm very appreciative of that.

Although I don't require nor expect such generosity just because I enjoy the sex anyway, such act of kindness is greatly appreciated. For Christmas 2005, Jeff gave me a card with $100 cash inside; in the following year, he gave me a Victoria's Secret lotion and perfume set; and before he left for Seattle in August 2007, he handed me a gold ring with Opals as parting gift.

Jeff never spoke openly about why he was so attracted to me. I think the majority of straight-but-curious men are like that. They are better off not talking about it or being asked about it. I totally respect that.

My relationship with these straight men is mutual, I would say. They respect me for who I am, and in return, I respect their most safely-guarded secrets. It is undeniable that I am beginning to relish my time with these faces in the dark. The feeling of being a sex deviant is starting to dissipate. For some strange reason, I am enjoying my time with these "devils" and "demons". I am having one hell of a time!

I get burned, too, sometimes.

Rick Mikhailovich

Coming from the scenic hills of the Salinas-Monterey border is a handsome, fifty year-old widower named Rick Mikhailovich. He is an architect and a part-time contractor. With him, I had nothing but the best and most memorable experiences.

He treated me like a very special lady when we were together. He prepared sumptuous meals for me, bathed me in eucalyptus and other fragrant oils, and pleased me like no other lover could. We even slow-danced to the songs of Angie Stone and Yolanda Adams once; with the lights dimmed. It was very romantic and *diabolique!* Once again, I found myself dancing with the devil. I simply didn't know him well.

I met Rick in the fall of 2004 through the popular website Craigslist. He responded to my *Casual Encounter* posting; looking for a brand new friendship and hopefully, some romantic adventures. He had just been widowed the previous year; his beloved wife, Lenita, died of cancer in December 2003.

I felt Rick needed companionship and meaningful conversations. I was there to fill in those requirements. All I wanted was to help him get through with the healing process in some way. We seemed to get along really well.

For two months Rick and I were in good, happy terms. Every weekend, I would drive some close to 50 miles to be with him. He would cook me dinner and we would have a pleasurable time afterwards.

Sometime in December 2004, the winds of passion changed their course. Rick realized he couldn't go on with our relationship anymore, owing to the fact that he felt he was dishonoring the memory of his beloved wife.

Being an understanding person, I accepted his decision. Deep inside me though, I was devastated.

It would take months before I completely recovered from the break-up. Reality could be a relentless enemy, that's for sure. Over time though, I learned to accept the fact and ultimately stopped asking myself why.

Ken Schumacher

In the spring of 2005, I am totally *over* Rick Mikhailovich. Enter Ken Schumacher: another middle-aged divorce` who lives in the Oakland Hills. A good-looking single father of two boys and a part-time masseur, Ken was one of those *DILFs* (Daddies I'd Like To Fuck) who really turned me on big time.

The awesome massage he would give me is the constant icing to the cake of our dates. He leaves me in a euphoric state after every meeting. One Sunday evening in the spring of 2005, when I felt very exhausted because of too much work in and out of the house, Ken invited me over and gave me what was to become the best massage I've ever received.

Ken and I would also soak ourselves up in his spa and would do the *dirty deed* there. We didn't care at all about the voyeurs and other nosy neighbors who might be secretly watching; rather we just cared about pleasing each other.

The spa pool scene would duly remind me of the many nasty sessions I've had with a bunch of men at the Grand Central Spas in San Jose. While Ken teases my face with his sexy, round behind, I couldn't help but imagine the past lovers I had who would do the same thing to me while half soaked in the hot tub. I had some very kinky visualizations—"apparitions of asses" as I coined them—and I loved it. Physically, it was Ken's butt in front of me, but in my mind, it was Kyle's, Kent's or Kirk's.

In May 2005, a few days after my 28th birthday, Ken and I met for the last time. As a birthday gift, he handed me some orchids in a porcelain pot. Those orchids were some of the most beautiful I have ever seen.

After that May meeting, I did not hear from Ken anymore. There was no response to my e-mails and no return calls either.

Sad as it may seem, the only consolation I have is the fun, sexy memories and the beautiful orchids he gave me.

"You can't please everybody," the saying goes. I never intended to. From then on, I vowed to be more careful when it comes to choosing the men whom I'd meet, greet and *eat*.

CHAPTER SIX

Sexy Druggies and Alcoholics

It was a high and dry feeling. "Damn! This is good!" I told myself. I didn't want it to stop. I wanted to cum so bad. This is how I felt after Michigan-native and trucker, Dave of San Jose, enticed me into doing *crack* one September night in 2004 when he called me for a massage appointment. He didn't really need a massage though. He just wanted some good butt massage.

Dave was a blond-haired, blue-eyed truck driver in his late thirties. He was a single white guy with a passion for Asian transsexuals. He also loves bragging about his sexy behind with a boyish grin, declaring "women enjoy holding on to it."

Well, I was luckier than those women because I got to do all *kinds* of things with it.

I was all over his ass once we made it to his tiny makeshift room inside the shed he was renting along Monterey Road. I admit, it was pure trailer-trash experience: Dave the horny white guy and myself, the filthy, nasty, willing, cash-for-cock whore.

Unfortunately for me that night, the *softening* effects of coke took its toll. I was not able to *release* that night. What made things worse was a phone call from Dave's boss, ordering him to do a late-night tow in Fairfield.

"Goddamn it! I need to cum!" I told myself.

We had no choice but to part ways. Dave promised he'd call again, but just like any other "first date," it never happened. It's a cliché. It was my first *and* final meeting with that sexy blue-eyed devil.

A couple of months after my encounter with Dave—in November 2004—I hooked up with another good-looking *snortee*, Marcellus of Benicia. We met at a hotel in Fremont. My brand new lover-for-the-night paid for the room and I was not to disappoint him. The least I could do was show him how nasty and kinky I could be in the bedroom. I knew very well it would excite any man I become intimate with.

The hotel maid was probably cursing out a barrage of *"puta madre!"* nonstop while cleaning our room after we left. It was a huge mess—bed sheets wet with *all* kinds of bodily fluids and liquid (beer), and chairs and tables in a state of disarray that one would think Naomi Campbell or Russell Crowe had stayed there the night before.

Marcellus was about ten years younger than Dave; tall, dark and handsome. He had Mediterranean features. I bet your *hummus* Marcellus was of Greek descent. He was nice and friendly and had a very big dick—almost 9 inches. He had swinger tendencies because while we were at it, he even called his girlfriend to tell her he was having a great time.

Unlike my encounter with Dave though, my time with Marcellus was a sexually-satisfying one. I reached orgasmic stage twice and my host was nice enough to let me pass out in his hotel room. He was considerate enough not to let me drive while intoxicated and under the influence. At least I knew he cared.

Around the same month, I met with an average-looking but very generous *dealer*, John of Martinez, CA. Originally a massage client, our session turned out to be one of the most erotic and unforgettable I've ever had.

Prior to our meeting, John was honest enough to confess that he was a drug dealer, but all he wanted was a massage. Having a reputation for being fair and non-judgmental towards people—as long as they're nice to me—I agreed. John rented a room at my favorite hotel in Fremont.

Surprisingly, John was just your average Joe: nice and normal. We talked about a lot of things, from sports to sweepstakes. The best part of that encounter was the fact that John was just plain respectful and giving.

After some ten to fifteen minutes of lively conversation, John asked permission if he could "light some up." Of course, I agreed. At that point, I realized we were just two consenting adults, not a masseuse-client tandem anymore. All I cared about was giving and getting pleasure. He then took out his paraphernalia and worked his magic like a bona fide snake charmer.

After a couple of hits, the "heavenly" effects started dominating my senses. I was on cloud nine. John was my god and I, his worshipper. I did every thing he told me to do in the name of fun, pleasure and money.

At the end of our session, he handed me $300 in cash and thanked me for being "such a cool person." John never realized that ironically, I had a blast with him.

I recently met up with John after almost seven years of estrangement. He looked better and seemed to be headed towards a better direction in life. After serving time in jail as a result of his felonious drug activities, he is now "clean and sober." He is even planning to marry a girl from the Philippines that he met online and settle down. I could only wish him the best of luck. I hope this new bitch is not only after a Green Card and that she won't bring new troubles in John's life.

Recalling my very first encounter with him and the complaints he had about some whores and hookers he met in the past, I could very well sum up that he had terrible experiences with them; that I was a breath of fresh air to him. I might have been a bitch to him, but in a good, kinky and sexy way. You get what I mean, don't you?

JC is perhaps the king of all *horndogs*, druggies and alcoholics. I never saw him sober. He was nice alright, but never sober. Yes, he is a walking crack pipe but definitely one of the nicest and most generous individuals I've ever met. After meeting a bunch of bad guys and cheapskates in the early years of my being a wild T-girl, JC was a cool breeze of fresh air. And the air smelled like brand new, crispy one hundred dollar bills!

JC is a divorce` from San Jose who works at a law firm in Cupertino, CA. From December 2000 up until the early part of 2003, we dated. Ours had been a sexual relationship cemented by twenty, fifty and one hundred dollar bills. JC didn't mind giving me money and I, in turn, was most welcoming to the idea. At the time, I didn't have a stable job and had to struggle to support myself.

JC was my rescuer. Whenever he would invite me over, he'd shower me with lots of money. All he ever wanted was my precious time and company. I was there to give it to him.

The sex was a one-way street commitment. I had to give and give. Sometimes I'd be *servicing* him till the wee hours of the morning. I didn't mind. As the song "Private Dancer" goes, *"You keep your mind on the money; keeping your eyes on the wall."*

JC was notorious for drinking can after can of beer and snorting coke at the same time, while dirty movies were playing. That was his personal heaven. That scenario really made him feel good. He was "king" of his own little world filled with sex, drugs and alcohol. He had it going on. I've never met anyone who'd level to JC's "partying" nature. I mean, we're talking about a marathon of sex, drinking and coke-snorting for hours straight.

Sometimes he'd call me up for two consecutive nights. Regardless, he'd still compensate me for my time. I had no complaints at all. To JC, money was no object.

I was young and wanted to experiment and explore. In the back of my mind, I enjoyed my romps with JC. I was benefiting from it financially. It helped improve my living situation.

The last time I saw JC was in April 2003. I just got back from my Philippine trip. By then, I was having a change of heart; maybe because I was also involved in a serious relationship with my then-boyfriend, Jon. The idea of cheating on my boyfriend seemed to have dominated my mind. I just thought it was not the right thing to do. When the spring season ended that year, so did my late-night meetings with JC.

Wherever he is now, I wish him the best and I also hope that he has changed for the better. Too much drugs and alcohol is not good.

Poppers make me hornier, no doubt. I consider it an "enhancer." I become more kinky and nasty during sex every time I take a whiff. My forty-something married lover, Bob Simms, always have some handy. Bob and I met in early 2005 and since then, he has been a regular visitor of mine at the hotel where I hang out.

Bob's expression of affection towards me is outstanding. His lines of "I love you" and "Daddy loves you" are endless, whether by phone or e-mail. He is one of the sweetest guys around.

Bob would always bring poppers and would periodically inhale it while we're having sex. I always have a great, satisfying time with him. Bob is very good-looking and very giving as well. He ensures my happiness in the bedroom. I couldn't ask for more. Well, maybe some *more* of those poppers.

CHAPTER SEVEN

Twinks & Other Teen Lovers

I n my personal diary, I wrote about my relationships and trysts with some young men, but unintentionally missed one beautiful subject. John Carrington was a Mountain Range High grad like my self. He was from the class of 1999. In 1996, he was just a freshman and I was already a senior. We never crossed paths though. Maybe we did, but back then my full attention was directed towards Tyler, Bill, Dave, Shawn, John, Jeremy and Benji. During those days, John was *just* a boy, not worthy of my attention and appreciation yet.

John and I won't cross each other's paths until after some seven years, when he was already a gorgeous, handsome young man.

In 2003, John was already a college student in San Diego, but was back in the Bay Area for Winter Break. Previously, we had been communicating through the internet and that weekend in February, we agreed to rendezvous near his house.

This tall, good-looking blond, with the looks of an Abercrombie & Fitch model, had no idea I attended the same high school where he went, although I think he knew from the very beginning that I was a transsexual. I suppose his curiosity prevailed, leading to his decision to have sexual experiences with a different gender besides the female kind.

On my part though, I thought it was just a one-time encounter. Little did I know that John would want more than just a one night stand with me.

Our first meeting took place at the Walgreens parking lot along El Camino Real and Grant Road in Mountain View, CA in February 2003. It was a meeting that would serve as a precursor to the many exciting sexual encounters we would share for the following years.

The majority of our meetings took place in my car. Most of the time, we ended up parking at one of El Camino Hospital's half-filled, dark lots, including the Emergency area.

Recalling one of those steamy scenes with a sense of humor, I'd say John and I had some sort of a "sexual emergency" that night; that my young lover needed some kind of immediate *attention* soon.

John, although *straight* as an arrow, never hesitated to bend the rules of masculinity. His softer side is often revealed when he moans passionately while I give him what could be the best blow job he is receiving. Whenever I hear him moan and see him climax, I'd assume he doesn't really care anymore about what the world thinks; only the "oohs" and "ahhs" that are in perfect harmony serve as his response. "I don't give a fuck" would be what's on John's mind, I'd assume; or "I'm in heaven!"

Whether we do it in my car or in a hotel room, John's orgasms are some of the most intense one could ever witness. He is never shy to show it. All these sensations are heightened when I use my big tongue on him; he shakes and shivers in the sexiest manner. Of course, the crowning moment takes place when my boytoy lies on his back so comfortably, with his elbows up, like a blond Viking being pleased by one of his captive whores. What an amazing sight. I love every second of it.

Once done, he takes a shower, towels himself dry, lies down for a few minutes and asks for a foot rub; after which he would rise, put his clothes back on, give me a hug and bid good-bye.

Conversely, John is also a giving lover. Like my former boytoy, Carl, he makes sure I get my satisfaction. I like having him sit on top of me and treat me like a horsey-horsey ride. That is pure *heaven*; although it's not the moon and stars that I see, rather a gorgeous pair of "golden globes" hovering up and down.

It's been five years since John and I first met and to this day, I still look forward to seeing this handsome hunk walk in, undress and lay his body down for my *eating* pleasure. Even though our meetings are only for a short period of time, at least I know the memories will last for a lifetime.

John is only a small dot in my Boytoy Blackbook though. For the past eight years of my being a wild T-girl, I also had the wonderful opportunity of meeting other sexy and good-looking eighteen and nineteen year-old California hunks. Here are some of the shining stars of those unforgettable nights: Trevor (a one time Orange Julius employee) and Pete (an aspiring rocker), both from San Francisco; John Powers of San Mateo, Jesse Bacchus of Redding, Rob (who drives a dark blue VW Jetta) of Los Altos, Tom Fergus (aspiring Navy Seal) of Los Gatos, Aaron Sanfifer of Roseville, Avi of Belmont, Eddy of Novato, Adam Romo (who went to see Spider-Man 1 with me back in 2002), Jason Lee, Monty, Scott (who drives an older model white Acura Integra) and Nick Hobridge (who used to play for the basketball team of SJSU), all from San Jose; Johnny of Moraga (who used to play for the football team of a college in Lafayette), Mike of Campbell, Chris Waker of Livermore (who drives a white Ford 150 pick up truck), Jon Long of Concord (who was nice enough to take me out to dinner at the Elephant Bar), Aaron Martel of Stockton, Anthony Kalidon of Hayward, John Corinthia (US Navy) of Sonoma, Sean of Van Nuys (whose father is a prominent Hollywood producer), Eric of Riverside (who accommodated me at his UC campus apartment for one night), Ernie Phillip of Fremont, Chris of Santa Clara (skater guy who used to work at the Senior Center), Michael Media of San Jose (eighteen year-old Pokemon fan whom I picked up near the Valley Fair mall), Freddy and Jason Henders, both from Sunnyvale; Will Cuesta of Daly City, Chris of Emeryville (who likes to smoke pot before sex) and Randy of San Jose (Atrium Gardens resident and self-proclaimed "Fighting Irish" because of his penchant for soliciting fights).

I also had some steamy encounters with young men joining the military for the first time. Let's just say I gave some of them their much deserved "farewell kiss." We did it on the eve of their deployment. I particularly enjoyed my encounters with Brandon of Sunnyvale, CA and the aforementioned Tom Fergus of Los Gatos. I'll never forget their rosy complexion and the smoothness of their pubic areas. They were hot, hot, hot!

I met Brandon in the summer of 2004. He was a good-looking kid with fairly good plans for his future. He was really into joining the US Navy. It was the height of the Iraq War and like many young men at the time, Brandon had a bad case of "9/11 Fever." He wanted to avenge America. He had dark blond hair and baby blue eyes and a big, fat dick. I remember sweating like a pig while we were doing it in the backseat of my Oldsmobile. It was both pleasure and pain.

I had to move my car three times though. I saw a couple of his neighbors turn their front porch lights on which immediately gave me the warning that they knew something fishy was going on. Their suspicions were genuine because inside my Oldsmobile it was Brandon's fat *pink salmon* that was slapping its way all over my face and working its way inside my tight *canal*. It was kind of humorous in a way but no doubt memorable.

Wherever they are now, I hope they're still alive and that their arms and legs are still attached to their hunky bodies.

The nights I shared with these young men are definitely unforgettable. How could you forget their soft and smooth pinkish complexion; their stupid, silly remarks; their strapping young asses and boyish grins, and their sexy, musky scent? Maybe if I were a nun I would. But I'm *not*. I am Kiki Malachite and I am every mother and girl friend's worst nightmare.

Chapter Eight

Deep Pockets, Hot Shots and Gentlemen

"Hey, big spender! Spend a little time with me"—Shirley Bassey

"Thank you for the *gift*, Joe, Bill, Mike, John . . ." The list goes on. I always have a great time with my kind, handsome and rich lovers. It's a fact. Ask me how I acquired my monetary and material possessions—my Mercedes, my dazzling gold and diamond jewelry and hefty bank account—and the answer lies in this chapter.

Some people say I acquired my riches through nonstop whoring, some say it's because my eyes and lips are so inviting; some say it's through my charm and charisma, and some say I'm just one attractive, sexy, moneymaking mama. Whatever it is, all I can say to those people is that I worked hard for every penny in my pocket. "I have nothing to offer but blood, toils, tears and sweat," Winston Churchill once said. Please allow me to echo his sentiment because it is so applicable to my past experiences.

In this chapter, I thank and honor the few good (and generous) men who have supported me financially throughout the years.

Scott Anderson of Connecticut tops the list of my handsome lovers with deep pockets and genuine hearts. I couldn't ask for more. Every time we'd meet for a hotel date whenever he visits California, not only he'd order room service for me, but there's always a couple of hundred dollar bills waiting for me by the lamp table inside his nice suite. He prefers to stay at the Cypress Hotel in Cupertino, CA.

Scott is a very good-looking "daddy". He has that "teddy bear" build—the meaty, thick kind. He is just perfect. I like his smile, too—boyish yet warm and sincere.

Mike Remo of Dublin, California is another generous, forty-something friend of mine who never ceases to show appreciation whenever our schedules allow us to meet. One simple request of his is that I give him a nice, long and soothing massage which I don't mind at all.

Chris Bobbs is an Associate Publisher of a local magazine in San Jose and a long-time friend and lover. He is a very good-looking, baby-faced thirty-something hotshot. Despite his elevated rank in the social circles of San Jose, he still possesses a humble heart. He is never judgmental. He was never a "high-brow".

More importantly, he has great taste.

Out of all the beautiful transsexuals in the Bay Area, Chris chose me to be his lover and friend: an average-looking T-girl. Why? I don't know? Maybe because I don't steal his wallet or take advantage of his spending capabilities. He knows from the get-go that I am no gold-digger. I can afford to buy my own gold—in cash—mind you!

Why Chris chose me to be his favorite companion, god only knows. But I am thankful to god for giving me the opportunity to meet and know this wonderful guy. The thousands of dollars Chris has given me over the years have helped me improve my living situation.

Eddy Marquez is another forty-something friend of mine, also from San Jose. He is of Hispanic descent with average looks but with an exceptionally generous heart.

Like Mike Remo, he craves for a Saturday evening companionship and conversation. He is a divorce` with a nineteen year-old son.

Eddy would rent a nice hotel suite in San Jose and order room service for us. I always have a relaxing time with him. He makes me feel comfortable and in return, I make him feel good. It's a perfect combination.

When it's time to part ways, Eddy would hand me a couple of hundred dollar bills and thank me for my time.

I feel like the luckiest girl on earth because not only I get special treatment, I also receive "blessings" constantly. Some women go home like used rag dolls after their Saturday or Friday night *sexcapades* with their partners or the guys they've hooked up with at the club, but not me. Even if *this* rag doll goes home used and dirty, she goes home with a heavy pocket and an irreplaceable smile on her face. I'd get out of my car, walk towards my apartment building and shout out "Eat your heart out, Raggedy Ann!" while waving my hundred dollars bill in the air.

I am very smart when it comes to dating. I only go out with the best and the nicest. You won't find me chasing asses at clubs like what other people do. Men come to me, not the other way around.

Wayne Livermore is one of the sweetest, most generous lovers I have. He's in his early fifties but does not look his age at all. Such boyish looks! I think the dimples on his cheeks add to his youthful appearance. He is probably a police officer or some Immigration agent because he is so secretive and discreet about his job. Never talks about it. Once he just rebutted with a grin when I asked him about it. I got the hint from the get go, so naturally, I'd follow Alice Keppel's rule: discretion is a must.

Wayne loves my dirty talk in the bedroom. It drives him crazy and makes him *release* in the most sexy and sensual way. He would blurt out the lines "You are a nasty whore! You are a nasty whore!" as he reaches climactic stage. As we savor the after moments of our lovemaking though, he'd follow up with the sugary line "You are a whore, but a good kind of whore."

In the back of my mind I just tell myself "Yeah, yeah, yeah! Now give me my money, daddy."

Keani Davidson of San Mateo is originally from Hawaii; hence, the tattoos on his back featuring the islands of Hawaii and his tanned complexion. He moved to California some five years ago and in early 2006, we met and became good friends and lovers. Apart from being a good friend and lover, he is also very generous. After our time together, he would hand me a long white envelope with money inside.

He likes going to the beach. He also enjoys shopping for women's clothes in San Francisco.

Keani has a penchant for cross-dressing. There are times when he would bring women's clothing to the hotel where I stay and would model them for me. It's his *therapy*. I am never bothered by it. In my mind, if he is open-minded enough to accept me for being me, I should treat him the same way. He is a nice and caring person and that's the only thing that matters to me.

Discretion is *definitely* a must though. I suppose one important factor—if not the most important reason—why these gentlemen choose to keep me is because of the fact that I always keep my mouth shut once I leave their hotel room and bedrooms. I tell myself "we are lovers in private and strangers in public." That's another "business" rule I quietly yet effectively enforce.

CHAPTER NINE

Bed, Butts and Beyond

From time to time, while combing the pages of this book, you would read about "the hotel" in Fremont, CA and my *sexcapades* there. It's my favorite "hang-out" spot. It's where fun and kinky things happen. I get so excited when I think about this place. I consider this place a second home, and my rented room—or my "raunchy room"—as my second bedroom.

Whether I use it for work or for play, I have to make sure my guests are comfortable. At the present time, the daily rate is about $45. You can't beat that. It's one of the cheapest, most practical hotels to go to, especially if you're on a tight budget; and if you're on the prowl for a sexy tight man butt.

The location is discreet: nestled along a frontage road near the 680 freeway. My friends, admirers and lovers have continuously complimented my choice of location; that it is a "nice" place to meet.

Of course, I know they are bullshitting me. I know deep inside them it is a *great* place to meet. They tell me it's nice because god knows they wouldn't want to be caught or seen by coworkers, relatives, wives and girlfriends entering the premises of a hotel so visible to the public. This hotel is their hidden playground.

All three managers respectively—the flirtatious Turkish-born Nazzi, the very nice Vic and the cordial Kevin—were very good to me. I couldn't ask for more. We had a harmonious manager-customer relationship. Whatever complaints or comments I had, they entertained and resolved. I really appreciate that. Nazzi even asked me out on a date once.

At any rate, I have been a loyal customer of that hotel since 2003.

On Tuesday and Saturday afternoons, I would check in. Once in my designated room, I lay out my armada of make up essentials: eye brow pencil, mascara, lipstick, liquid foundation, loose powder and blush on. The lipstick and mascara are my favorite "magic wands." They create magic for me. They give me beauty. They transform my looks from girl-next-door to big-time and big-earning sexy whore. I love it!

Once my face is done, I am ready to face the world—or a bunch of asses sticking high up in the air for that matter.

But first, I look in the vanity mirror, beam a naughty smile and utter the lustful line "Mirror, mirror on the wall, who's the nastiest of them all?"

And the show begins.

I find it highly erotic to think that I went through time and trouble in putting up an immaculately made up face only for it to be messed up by my lovers' big, sexy, protruding body parts. I love it though. It's a huge turn on. It feels good to be near men's *assets*. I fancy myself as the best *asscort* around. Naughty, isn't? It is, but the men aren't complaining, so why should I.

Personally, all the teasing from those male body parts—and the orgasm that follows—are my most effective form of therapy. It makes me feel so good inside and out. It's as simple as that. I feel so relaxed afterwards.

The positive effects are not only internal. Not too long ago I went through old personal photographs taken in the early 2000s and compared them with recent ones. There is a considerable amount of difference: my face looks fresher these days than seven or eight years ago. Maybe those squirting cocks have served as my "fountains of youth." Regardless, I am happy with the results. Who needs botox when I can get my own *boytox?*

Often times I run out of fresh towels. Not to worry. My marvelous maids are at my beck and call. Thanks to Annie, Lacy and Nadri. They make sure I get my basic hotel essentials. These ladies are truly my *maids of honor.*

They are constantly rewarded, of course. A couple of times a month and on Christmases for sure, I would hand them nice tips. They truly deserve it.

That hotel is my own "Ali Baba cave". In it, I've acquired all my riches and monetary possessions, much thanks to my loyal lovers who have continuously patronized my companionship over the years.

It's my own "secret garden"; a place where wonderful things happen.

Alluding the hotel to Ali Baba's magical cave only reminds of my Arabian lover from Fremont—Mani—and the lustful words I'd use when sending him text messages each time I summon him:

> *"Mani, Mani, open sesame, Mani!*
> *Open your man-cave nice and wide for me, Mani!!"*

Some of you might find it outrageous, but those are the exact words I use when inviting my Arabian lover to come over; no more, no less.

Not all my experiences in that hotel are as exciting and stimulating as those stories found in the *Arabian Nights.* Life is not a bowl of candies and cherries at all. I know this for a fact.

My very own eyes have been witness to rejection and discrimination, too.

There were a few occasions when some of the men I was meeting for the first time walked out of my hotel room as quickly as they had entered. Why, I do not know.

But in the back of my mind, I knew I was not their *type*; that my physical appearance did not meet their expectations.

I am not petite at all. I don't have a slim figure either. To some, I am beautiful; to some, I am just of average looks. But one thing I know very well, I am just me. I am happy and content with my looks, and I don't give a rat's ass about other people's standards and "expectations".

"Keep your money, shove it up your stinking ass and go to hell!" is what I'd tell those rude men.

When those few men walked out on me as soon as they saw me, I didn't feel belittled or rejected at all, rather I was glad I didn't have to waste time on such despicable human beings.

I make sure there is not a single fiber of their hatred and indifference left in my room. As soon as they walk out and I slam the door on them, I take a deep breath and let positive thoughts reign in my mind again. Soon, excitement fills the air, for I know pretty soon there will be *heavenly* joy for me.

The fun continues. I could never exactly recall the many times Mike, Andrew, Neil, Matt, Mark R, Bob, Bill, Chris, Mark A, Nate, Kevin, Greg, Marty, John, and my other loyal lovers have visited me and made me happy and *satisfied*. Call it excess, call it debauchery but never call it boring. The years 2005, 2006, 2007 and 2008 are some of the best years of my sexual life.

I am one hot, kinky and oversexed sexy mama and I love it!

The *show* must go on, and so should the fun and excitement. It's my life. It's my party. I'll make it last for as long as I want to, for as long as I can.

Maybe when I am old and withered, I might charter a limo and ask to be driven along Reservoir Avenue, where the hotel is located. I see myself glancing at that very special hotel with a resigned smile on my face, proudly murmuring the line, with teeth or no teeth, "Damn, I'm good!"

CHAPTER TEN

Something Beautiful Remains

In this great, big world we live in, feelings of unrequited love are dime a dozen. They go unnoticed most of the time. Time leaves them behind, people forget about them and the memories fade away. In my case, I would not want that to happen. Years will pass and the world will forget me, but in this book, the memories I have with the two most wonderful men I've met many years ago—Mark Aldredge and Jim Ragen—shall live on.

Open my heart and there is only one name you'll find—Mark Aldredge. He is the one true love of my life; the one man whose memory is so strong that sometimes I find myself waking up late at night, asking myself 'Why?'; whose sweet kiss I will never forget and will forever savor.

It's been five years since I last saw him, but the *fire* is still there. I believe you only discover your one and only true love once it has left you, not while it is near you.

I still long for Mark, I admit. There are nights when I'd wake up only to find myself thinking of him and desiring him. There are times when I'd look at another man and see in him physical qualities that remind me of Mark—the eyes, the hair and other things. There are moments when another man is making love to me and I'd whisper Mark's name at the apex of the pleasure I am receiving. There are nights when I'd dream about him and shed a tear once I wake up, realizing it's just my mind playing tricks on me.

When all of this longing would fade and disappear, I could only guess.

The love I felt for Mark continues to enslave me. From time to time, he is in my thoughts. If Neil Sedaka sings "Breaking Up is Hard to Do," for Mark, my heart bemoans "letting you go was a hard thing to do." I miss him terribly.

Maybe someday I'll learn to walk along the sunlit hallway of my house and not tell myself "Here's another day of longing for the real sunshine of my life—Mark Aldredge" anymore.

But, something beautiful remains: the love that I will always have in my heart. Well, at least, I'm one of the few people in the world who knows the meaning of true love—because it lives and thrives in my heart.

Not far from where Mark lives—in beautiful San Francisco—is my one and only "Daddy Jim." The experiences I had with this very special man are stuff that romance novels are made of. I am so proud to have had those experiences.

Forever I will cherish the good times and happy moments we've shared. I am wholly content with the fact that I am one of the few who had been fortunate enough to experience Daddy Jim's love and kindness. Although we don't see each other anymore, my heart is not sad and bitter. I could only wish him all the happiness this ever changing world has to offer.

CHAPTER ELEVEN

It's What I Do Best

This chapter is not for the faint at heart. If you're not as sexually charged and confident as I am, I suggest you stick to reading the sex articles of *Glamour* or *Cosmopolitan.* They're for the novice.

A lot of you might wonder how I am able to keep up with so many men. I suggest you rephrase the question and ask "Why do men keep coming back to you?" instead.

I am not the Oracle at Delphi. I am only human; a very unique and talented one though. I don't have great words of wisdom, but when it comes to pleasing a man—and Final Jeopardy—I know damn well I do a very good job.

Great skills, dexterity and talent—you have to have these.

If Picasso was master of the paintbrush, Kiki Malachite is the mistress of pleasuring.

"Love is blind," the saying goes. I say "Learn to love a man's behind!" Men will always come back for more and more pleasures in the bedroom, that's for sure. You have to realize that sex is as important to him as food. A regular five-minute blow job you give him is never enough.

I don't need a scientific theory to back up this bedroom concept. I am not a scientist, just a *sexualist*. From the many men I've met, dated and gone to bed with, I have all the confidence in the world to declare that I *know* men very well. Experience *is* everything.

Men want more than just a mere blow-job. Men have an insatiable appetite for anything sexual, whether it's oral pleasure, masturbation or intercourse. In reality, a man likes *all* of his genitals touched, caressed, kissed, licked, tongued and pleased. Pleasuring a man does not start and stop in giving him a blow-job. For someone to say a mere blow job is enough for a guy, that person must be a teenager.

What's good for the gander is good for the goose. But sometimes the gander doesn't get all the "good stuff" he deserves. And when that happens, Kiki comes to the rescue. I give my men 101% satisfaction, or as how this popular auto supply store puts it, I "go the extra mile." What their wives and girl friends fail to give them in bed, I provide.

Truth is, he might not tell the wife or girl friend upfront that he likes his ass licked or toes sucked just because it might provoke a sense of disgust (on the latter's part); but it won't hurt for his significant other to try.

I could never recall the number of occasions when I've pleased a man and did not hear him moan like a whore, for lack of a better term. No offense to the men, just a mere comparison. After all, we *are* all whores in the bedroom: we serve and we get served and *serviced*. It's an endless cycle. It's being human!

Let the fun begin. Picture me kneeling down the floor while my lover is lying on his back on top of the bed, in a "spread-eagle" position. I would then start caressing his inner thighs and the sides of his crotch with my sexy long nails, and simultaneously kiss the back of his knees and thighs with my sexy red lips.

I haven't touched his penis at this point, but I can see he is oozing wet.

Also at this point, his "hard on" is visible. Surely the teasing I gave him had had a stimulating effect.

I would then proceed a little "higher" (this means I am leveling my face to that of his crotch area) and begin blowing kisses into his balls and give them some occasional licking. All the while, my fingers are flirting with his ass crack.

After some two or three minutes of more teasing, I would then use my left hand and start stroking his penis. But the teasing *from* the right hand doesn't stop. It goes on and on. Remember, I'm giving my man 101% satisfaction. I want to do *things* right. I really believe if I weren't a *sexualist*, I'd be a professional piano player today. I have such good, nimble fingers!

Did I mention I am also a sex machine? You probably know that by now. Keep on reading, please.

At this point, both my hands are functioning and my mouth has started kissing on my man's balls, asshole and the sides of his crotch. Light, gentle kisses at first and gradually they become more intense and wild.

Soon, I will be using my big, fat tongue. I'd be licking my lover's ass crack up and down, like an elevator, in a vibrating motion. I personally call it the "Elevator Ride". And no, I wouldn't mind giving Noah Wyle one!

Oh yes, you've read about my tongue. Not only it is big and fat, it's also "wicked" (I quote a one-time lover, Mark Lindon, on that). Other lovers have called it "velvet", "magical" and "wonderful."

Move over, Gene Simmons! Kiki's big, fat, "magical" tongue is unstoppable.

Whenever I use my big tongue on men, Mozart's music seems to be playing in my ear. You might wonder what that means. I am talking about the moaning of these men. Such sweet music!

Not all women are capable of making their husbands and boyfriends moan in deep pleasure. I think some of them make their men yell and scream instead, with all the bitching and nagging they unleash.

A man should be given love and support constantly, and lots of pleasure. What some women don't know is that deep behind that strong, macho façade lies a sensitive soul; a soul that just like a flower, also needs some tending and gentle touch. That sensitive side is very well connected to a man's sexual nature.

Contrary to common beliefs, men love their ass cheeks and ass cracks touched and caressed gently with long nails. Men love their feet played with and toes kissed (or sucked, if you want to be extra naughty). Men love their nipples and stomach played with using gentle, feather-like caresses. Men love their legs and thighs rubbed and kissed. Men love the sides of their crotch kissed and licked. Men love being deep-throated and rimmed. My *MFFs* (married male friends) certainly enjoy these things.

To most of them, I am one-in-a-million. I may not have the beauty of a Miss Universe candidate—or the light complexion of that mediocre actress in the Philippines named Anne with whom many Filipinos are so crazy about—but I assure you, I have the sexual skills of a thousand courtesans combined; not to mention my oozing sex appeal. I really believe the majority of men opt for the latter qualities. This is simply a strong statement coming from a t-girl who has experienced it all; with good instincts and an even better intuition.

Also, I am not asking for long term, exclusive commitments, nor am I asking for a four-carat diamond ring. Hell no! I can afford to buy my own ring, mind you.

When it comes to having secret sexual relationships with my married male friends, I am absolutely one happy camper. Throw this sexy poodle a boner and she's happy!

So, I suppose my recurring question to those who disagree with this argument would be "What is beauty if the brain is devoid of nasty and kinky imaginations?" I don't think that's going to be fun. And we all know that bad sex in a marriage can lead to a bevy of marital problems and eventually, divorce.

Every time a lover visits me, I make sure I give him the best experience. And the best always comes out of each and every encounter.

I could never recall the many times I've *sent* those horny Johns and Jims to heaven with my extraordinary pleasing skills. To them, I am the epitome of a great lover. I possess powerful and effective pleasing skills. I am Kiki Malachite, bona fide *maneater.* Hear me purr!

CHAPTER TWELVE

Proud to be a Bad Girl

I'm a very kind, caring and compassionate person. I know that for a fact. Ever heard of the saying "You know yourself better than others"? That's very true. It is so applicable to me. I know myself better than anyone else.

I've bestowed thousands of dollars and innumerable acts of kindness on many people: friends, lovers and relatives. I have no regrets. I feel happy doing it. I feel complete as a person. After all, we're only travelers in this world. Sooner or later, our journey will end. The paths we take and the small steps we make will serve as a guide to future generations. Let's be good and kind to others.

But I am only human. I am not perfect. I can be a *nasty* girl, too. I have no regrets. I feel happy being that way. I feel complete as a very sexual human being when I do nasty things . . . in the bedroom. After all, I am an *adventurer*. I am the transsexual counterpart of Casanova—fast forward to the 21st century. I am absolutely proud of it. There's only one life to live. Remember that.

Brotherly Loving

From mid-2000 until the early part of 2003, I dated the Hassad brothers, Mike and Alex. These boys are of Middle Eastern descent. They have the biggest dicks I've ever seen.

I first met Mike through the internet. He was one of those early respondents to my Yahoo! Personals profile.

I never really paid too much attention to Mike at first. He was short, with average looks and a not-so-fit body. He was not my *type*. But he had a lot of money.

Finally, after several attempts to lure me into his crotch, I succumbed. Not without a hundred-dollar check for every meeting though.

Mike was about my age. He had a good-paying job. He seemed smart. He worked at a bank in Fremont, CA. He was very horny, too.

During the first few years of the new millennium, I had all the time in the world to do nothing. I was unemployed, too. The cash flow was limited. I am still very thankful to my Mom for supporting me, financially. I'll never forget her generosity. Because of that, I survived. I remember gathering coins—quarter dollars, nickels and dimes—and having them exchanged for one dollar bills at the local grocer.

Generous guys were a treat then. I reveled at the thought of men giving me money after my quality time with them. Who doesn't love money these days anyway? It was not prostitution though. Remember, I did not solicit money; the men voluntarily gave it to me. Let me be clear on that. It was something mutual rather. I never put a price tag for the time I spent with them. I was assuming the monetary gifts they gave me were a simple form of appreciation. I gladly accepted those "gifts".

Perhaps they thought the sex I gave them was so good that they had to give it justice. I'll never know. One thing I am sure of, I am very thankful for those *blessings*.

Mike Hassad belonged in the top ten list of the generous guys I've met in the early years of my wild T-girl days.

Whenever he craved for some *oral* attention, he called me and I was there for him. It didn't matter when or where: day or night, in my beat up Oldsmobile or his car, a hotel room or some isolated parking lot in Fremont.

It's a *dirty* job, but someone has to do it.

Alex—Mike's younger brother—was part of the "bonus" I sometimes gave Mike. I didn't mind that at all.

Men could be callous with their expenses sometimes and even the wisest money holder is vulnerable to bad spending. Whenever Mike couldn't come up with $100, he'd give me $80 or $60. That was fine with me.

Occasionally, Mike would make one bizarre request: give his younger brother, Alex, a blowjob.

So, after my meeting with Mike, I would then meet up with Alex. Alex would pick me up in his dark green Honda Accord and we'd park at some deserted or isolated spot in Fremont or nearby Hayward.

Alex was better-looking than his brother. He was younger, too. During those times, I was *into* younger men—those in their late teens and early twenties. Unbeknownst to Mike, I relished the fact that I'm *eating* his cute, younger brother. In other words, I didn't mind making my talented mouth do some "over time" work; or give some "freebie".

Alex was only nineteen at the time. He had a nicer build and a cuter face. Although not thoroughly handsome, he had more sex appeal. One thing Mike and Alex had in common was the fact that they both liked getting rimmed.

Alex would also make occasional requests such as a "booty shake" when I hop out of his dark green Honda Accord or maybe pull my *Daisy Dukes* shorts a little bit lower so he could have a peek of my healthy and sexy butt cheeks. I didn't mind. I liked Alex. He was a cool and nice guy.

On one occasion, we ended up doing the nasty at some residential street in Hayward near Industrial Parkway. It was very memorable because Alex actually got out of the car, stood by the driver side facing the door, stuck his cute butt out and let me do my thing. It was a daring move and I shamelessly obliged.

Hard to imagine that nobody saw us that night, but I didn't care at all. I was young and very adventurous. I wanted to be kinkier and try new things. I'm glad I did and am very proud of it.

The idea of being used by two brothers one after the other was a major turn on. I always have this recurring visual of myself appearing as a *cumster*.

The very idea that the Hassad brothers would just use my mouth whenever they feel like and get off good on it suits my wild and kinky imagination.

Mike stopped calling me in mid-2003. Why, I don't know. Maybe he got himself a girl friend or maybe he got married. Who knows?

It was my prerogative to stop entertaining Alex's phone calls after Mike decided to stop seeing me. It was fair game. Wherever those horse-hung boys are now, I just hope they're happy and that they're getting *it* from some bitch out there who is as kinky and nasty as me.

The Handy Men

Another group of men which I find sexy and exciting are construction workers and handymen. If you go back to one of the early chapters of this book, you'd read about a fantasy of mine involving gorgeous handymen like Evan Farmer and Jason Cameron (from *While You Were Out*) work on my house.

But then again, it's just a fantasy. Let's leave it like that. I am Kiki Malachite and I get what I want!

In the summer of 2006, the renovation of my spinster aunt's house in San Jose was well underway and by early 2007, ninety percent of the work had been done except for one more minor repair: the painting of the hallway wall.

One of the many contractors and handymen I've contacted was a young Hispanic male in his late twenties named Alizeo.

Alizeo was good looking and had a nice body. He resembled British-born Filipino actor Derek Ramsay. Alizeo had beautiful, sexy eyes. He had a charismatic tongue, too, matched by pretty lips; lips that were so irresistible. They were so irresistible that I wasn't able to control myself one January morning in 2007 and felt compelled to make out with him . . . after he pulled me closer to him.

He was doing a door-to-door routine that morning, advertising his services to residents in my aunt's neighborhood.

Alizeo hypnotized me with his very sexy gaze. He had some magic in him no doubt. After that meeting though, I did not commit to any work or repair. I had some other *job* in mind for him. Six months later, we were getting wild at a hotel in San Jose, CA. I'll never forget that.

In August 2007, I finally had Alizeo *working*. Room 1208 of the Holiday Inn was rented earlier that day by my massage client, Don Perrins. Don was a forty-something, Corvette riding, roof installer from Morgan Hill, CA. He decided to come to San Jose to get a massage from me that one hot August evening. He ended up renting a room at the Holiday Inn along Fourth Street.

After my session with Don, while driving home around 7pm, I received a phone call from Alizeo. He was cruising somewhere along Hostetter Avenue and had just finished work at a residence.

From the sound of Alizeo's voice, he was extremely excited. He wanted to see me badly.

"Where are you?" he asked with a slight Mexican accent. "I wanna *chee* you."

Then a bright idea came to my mind: Why not use the hotel room which Don had gotten earlier? He left me the key anyway.

I then instructed Alizeo to meet me at the Holiday Inn. He agreed.

After I hung up the phone, I made an abrupt U-turn from the street that I was driving on and hastily drove back to the hotel. I wanted to fix the bed and redo my make up before Alizeo came over. I wanted to look pretty for my new Latin lover.

I was craving for his *chorizo* badly.

By 8 o'clock that evening, Alizeo and I were in room 1208, getting to know each other better. He wanted something to drink though, so we went to a nearby 7-Eleven and bought some alcoholic treats.

Back at the hotel room, after a few bottles of Corona, Alizeo made the first move. He started kissing me and feeling my breasts. He liked making out, remember?

Soon after, he was making out with my sensitive brown nipples and as the minutes went on, he continued exploring my body with his strong hands and talented tongue, topping off our bedroom celebration with a good fuck.

He fucked me many times. It was so intense that I eventually became numb from the pain and pleasure. Alizeo was a wild *animal* in bed. He knew how to slowly punish and *devour* his captive. It was sexual torture filled with pleasure.

Alizeo was a very good lover. He knew how to take care of my *needs* despite the language barrier. Proof that when it comes to lovemaking, nothing really matters except the tongue and the *tool*.

In the end, I was so satisfied with the *work* done.

Before Alizeo though, another construction worker I met in the summer of 2006 was Irish-born Brendan Unden of San Mateo, California.

Brendan was a few years older than Alizeo, but he was just as good when it comes to having stamina. Another thing which made Brendan unforgettable was his great ass. He really looked good in blue jeans.

In July of 2008, I posted an ad on Craigslist's *Casual Encounter* section. I was bored. I wanted to have some *fun*. Brendan responded. He really looked good: ash blond hair, dark blue eyes, a fit body and a butt to die for. I suppose the luck of the Irish was working towards my favor that day. This Irishman's ass was better than any Guinness I had.

I guess I was really looking for an *asstimate*, not an estimate. Brendan gave me a good meal instead of a good deal.

Caught in the Act

In the spring of 2004, I started communicating with a handsome, middle-aged guy from Oregon. Don Carbonelli was of Italian-descent; tall, white and dark-haired, with an athletic physique comparable to that of a rugby player. He was the quintessential *DILF* (Dad I'd Like To Fuck). During those times, I fancied myself as a *sexplorer* and an adventurer. I wanted to try different things and be with different men, young or old. Don and I agreed that we would explore bondage and S&M sex upon our meeting. He had always been into the master and slave scene. In me he found a most qualified, eager and submissive bitch.

In April of that year, Don decided to visit the Bay Area. He wanted to meet me. He did not mind the long hours of driving. He felt it was totally worth it.

Don arrived on a Sunday. Coincidentally, I've made plans with another guy that day. Weeks before I started communicating with Don, I was already seeing Fred.

Fred, in contrast to Don, was a medium build, short and average-looking white guy. He offered good company though. Fred took me out dining at some of the Bay Area's finest restaurants. We had a nice time together. The chemistry was undoubtedly present. But I was *craving* Don more. On the same day that I was meeting Don, I made commitments with Fred.

It was a big mistake and a total miscalculation of things.

Upon Don's arrival at his hotel not far from my house, he called me on my cell phone to inform me that he was already in town, and that he was ready to see me. He sounded very eager to finally meet me.

I had to beg for some consideration from him though. At the time of his call, I was having early dinner with Fred at nearby Dave & Buster's.

I had to make up an excuse; a complete and utter lie. I told Don I was on my way to the Oakland Airport to pick up my brother, and that I won't be able to meet him right away. It was a terrible lie with equally terrible consequences.

Don, taking my word that I won't be able to see him until about 6 in the evening, decided to leave his hotel room to take a stroll inside the Great Mall of Milpitas. Coincidentally—and unfortunately—Dave & Buster's is located inside that mall.

After my early dinner with Fred, we decided to walk around the mall as well. Murphy's Law was definitely in full effect that afternoon. Although I did not see Don, apparently, he saw me with another man (without my knowledge).

The devastating and humiliating consequences did not occur at the mall, but rather at the hotel room where Don was staying. Around half past six that evening, I arrived at the hotel and formally introduced myself. I also *sincerely* expressed my apologies for meeting him that late.

Don was not convinced. He was visibly upset. His first lines were "Where did you say you were?"

As soon as he uttered those words I turned white like Liquid Paper.

"I'm sorry" was all I could say.

"I made time for you and drove for hours just to meet you and then you'll do this, you bitch!" he lashed out. Don's Italian temper had been ignited.

After several attempts to calm him down, Don became less irate. I did not hesitate a bit when it came to admitting that I lied to him. I explained that it was tough for me to decline a dinner date offered by a friend whom I have already met a couple of months earlier.

Seeing that I was contrite, slowly but surely, my explanations pacified Don.

"Alright, I forgive you, but you're still gonna be my bitch tonight," he said.

A few minutes later, Don unleashed a mighty combination sexual torture and verbal torment. I've never *eaten* so much man parts in a span of five minutes until that particular meeting with my handsome Italian sex master. He *fed* me what I truly deserved for being a nasty, two-timing and sex hungry tramp. It was such an embarrassing experience but in the end, everything turned out as originally planned: there was nasty, kinky sex.

The image of Don's healthy butt cheeks and big balls rubbing all over me surely served as the highlight to an erotic and eventful weekend. I *crave* for that kind of sex; something Fred was not able to provide.

I never heard back from Don again after that encounter. I didn't care anymore. I *got* my orgasm anyway. That's what matters! Honestly, I could've even given him gas money for his trip back to Oregon!

Men will come and go, I don't care. It's my *cumming* that really matters! Really!

Doing the nasty in Danville

Oh, yes. Let's not forget about the Sycamore Valley Road incident in Danville, CA. How could I forget? I got busted there by several cops in the summer of 2004. I was not alone when it happened though. I was with a handsome young white guy from Fairfield, CA.

Nate was twenty-two and very horny. On the night we met, I made a suggestion that we get a room. He refused.

I was feeling tired when I met him. I was dying to lay my body down on a comfortable bed.

A couple of hours earlier, I met with my other lover boy, Jon Michael, who lived a few exits down along that long stretch of interstate 680. I gave Jon some oral pleasures that night at a park somewhere along Alcosta Boulevard. It was such a hot scene. I sat him on top of the picnic table and had him spread eagle. I was *eating* him like there was no tomorrow. Now that's what I call a very satisfying "midnight snack."

Normally, after having my "midnight snack", I'd go to bed. That night was completely different. I decided to *eat* some more "white meat": Nate.

Nate, being the young, cheapskate, smart-ass college student that he was, ignored my plea for a hotel room. He insisted that everything will be fine. So, we decided to do *it* at a parking lot right off the Sycamore Valley Road exit along the 680 freeway in Danville. I remember there was a tennis court nearby.

It was a stupid move though. Even the horniest teenagers won't dare suck and fuck in such a well lit place. Regardless, I acquiesced.

As soon as Nate hopped in my beat up Oldsmobile (his car at the time was a small, dark-colored Chevrolet sedan, probably a Malibu), we started doing the nasty. After a few minutes, Nate *came* and I was catching my breath. I quickly pulled up my skirt and we started chatting. Suddenly, bright lights were beaming towards my car's windshield. *Uh-oh.* Soon, the siren of a CHP patrol car was resonating within the parking lot.

"Oh, shit!" was all I could say. Nate quickly pulled his pants up and sat upright.

After a few seconds, there was a knock on both sides; a cop on the passenger side window and another on the driver side.

"What are you guys doing here?" asked the cop on my side.

"We're just talking, officer," I replied.

"Can I see your license?" the cop on Nate's side asked him.

"I wanna see yours, too," the cop on my side interjected.

After a couple of minutes, both cops instructed us to get out of the car.

Nate was escorted near his car by two cops and I was told to remain on my seat while being questioned by another.

"Now, tell me, what were guys doing inside?" the good-looking but chubby thirty-something cop asked me.

And so my litany of explanations began.

"Ok officer, I'm sorry, we had sex. We first decided to just chat and one thing led to another. I didn't want to do it but he forced me and started to kiss me and feel me. He was forcing himself into me and I lost control, and to make him stop, I just decided to let him have his way."

The officer was probably surprised with my unabashed description and detailing of events; so he paused for a few seconds while looking at me straight in the eye.

"But you're not supposed to have sex in public places," he explained.

"I know that, officer. But he's a man, and I couldn't stop him. I'm sorry," I retorted.

"Ok, stay here. I'll get back to you."

Poor Nate. All I could hear was a barrage of curses and accusations being thrown at him. I really felt sorry for him. He was whiter than snow when I stole a glance.

The sight of this pitiful young man being verbally abused and threatened by grown up men was too much for me to bear. It was psychological torture. I was teary-eyed. But before a tear fell down on my face, here came Officer "Kevin James", telling me I shouldn't come to Danville at all if my only intent was to have sex in public. He then instructed me to get in my car and go home.

My final words to him were "Thank you, officer." I then sped away from the scene and never dared venture along that Sycamore Valley Road exit anymore . . . ever.

Sam Likes it Hot

Sam is a middle aged massage client of mine who is of Middle Eastern descent. He likes to reciprocate the massage that I give him. He is very good. Sometimes I think I should be the one paying him. He also has a penchant for my piss.

Our bodies are never perfect. *No* body is perfect! I know some men who have David-like physique (you know, that huge Renaissance sculpture by Michelangelo?) but have the body odor of a goat. Simply revolting! I know some men who smell so good you could mistake them for a bottle of *Axe* body spray, but then again the size of their bodies is astounding. Either way, I *love* them. I don't judge people by their outer exterior. Never! That is just shameful. You judge people by the way they treat you; not if you think they've eaten cans of *Treet* all their life.

So, I must confess, my body has its imperfections as well. There are mornings when I'd wake up and realize I have a zit here and there.

For some reason, after Sam and I are done with the massage session, he would ask me to piss on him. He has a penchant for *golden showers*. Sam likes my hot piss . . . a lot! Yes, he begs for it with complete alacrity.

He is just one hell of a nasty dirty old man! And I love it. As long as he's totally cool with it and gives me lots of *dough*, all I can say is "Sam, here you go!"

CHAPTER THIRTEEN

Sex in All the Bright Places

I am notorious for having sex everywhere. It doesn't matter if it's in the office, the bathroom, married men's bedroom, a college guy's bedroom, the garage, the attic, the basement, or the Laundromat. In fact, to cut down the chase, I am proud to say I've had sex on every freeway exit in the Bay Area: that includes exits along 101, 880, 280, 680, 580, 80 and 237. From Santa Rosa to Chula Vista, I've been a promiscuous travelling mama. Every time I drive along these freeways, kaleidoscopic visions of the men and my nasty activities with them appear. God Bless me for not getting into an accident! But then again I have such perfect control on almost everything, and that includes my driving!

Mike Cropley was a law-breaking lawyer I met in the fall of 2001. Ironic, isn't? Why? It's because he liked having sex in public places—with me. Don't you forget about those San Fernando Valley adult film producers, directors and actors who do their business on city streets and dark alleys. We're all *in* the business after all.

The reality is, sex is everywhere. Sometimes you see it happen, sometimes you don't. People do it in their bedrooms and hotel rooms, but sometimes they are daring enough to do it on the street or inside their cars and vans. You might not witness it all the time but you know damn well it is happening.

Take my experiences.

Some of my numerous sexual romps in the car took place in Palo Alto, California, at the parking lot of this law firm along Page Mill Road. Mike Cropley, a tall and handsome forty-something attorney, was both my passenger and lover.

Despite his generous salary due to his profession, in reality, he was a stingy person. He never bothered renting even the cheapest motel room for us. We have always done *it* in the backseat of my beat up Oldsmobile wagon.

Around 6 or 6:30 pm on certain days of the week, I would wait for Mike at the main parking lot. This is the time frame when most employees have left. Mike would take liberty in staying a little longer so he could feel my big, long tongue before he goes home to his girl friend. Sex with that woman was much worse than the stock market crash of '29, I guess. He complained nonstop about it.

Mike enjoyed my *bona fide* oral skills in pleasuring a man. He liked having his big, wide behind bombarded with kisses and licks.

Men's assholes, as a little FYI to you, my dear readers, are comparable to a clitoris: it is very sensitive and the slightest dab of a big, fat wet tongue would make men's toes curl in an instant. It's a fact. I know these things very well. Take it from the *sexpert*!

Some men love their *backdoor* entered; whether by tongue, finger or a dildo. This is a sexual standard most people do not know. Some men might deny it because of fear of embarrassment (that they might be looked upon by other straight men as fags and sissies with itching ass-*pussies*), but I assure you, most would agree to it.

All these kinky anal sex sessions took place within a period of 6 months. By early 2002, it was over. Apparently, Mike got hired by another law firm in Berkeley. Thus ending our car dates in Palo Alto.

The kinky activities I had with Mike Cropley did not begin and end with him. From the year 2000 and up until recently, I am proud to have had the following bizarre sexual experiences.

AOL member TenSevenOne (2000)

Originally an AOL "Online Buddy", this horny young college hunk decided to take our communication to a more personal level when he challenged me to meet him late at night at the Washington Mutual parking lot near my house. He wanted to see me do a "stripper-like dance." Being the daring person I am, I had no qualms about doing it.

Around 10:30 that one summer night, I drove to our chosen location and the minute I saw his tiny dark blue Chevrolet coupe park behind my car, I played Aerosmith's *Jaded*, got out of my car (wearing a black v-neck top with Playboy logo and black mini skirt), and danced in front of my awestruck admirer.

Anthony of Chevron on Santa Clara St. in Downtown San Jose (2001)

Stress and the need to *release* surely drove this twenty-something Latino gas station attendant to grope and grab me and rub his crotch on my butt cheeks one cold December night in 2001.

I was on my way home from dinner with a friend when I decided to stop by the Chevron gas station for a fill. Little did I know that I'd be experiencing a different kind of pumping.

As I was pumping gas into my Oldsmobile, someone groped me from behind and started humping me. I couldn't react and move right away because the man entangled himself on me so tightly. I was shocked and scared. When I got a chance to look at his face, I was astounded when I realized it was the gas station attendant.

"What the fuck are you doing?!?" I screamed. He didn't respond, rather he just continued rubbing his horny self all over me, assuming I was a blow up fuck doll with no feelings and reaction.

"You're sooo sexy baby," he whispered in my ear.

Anthony was rubbing his crotch on my buttocks uncontrollably. He was acting like a wild, sex-crazed man who had just gotten out of prison.

Finally, after a minute, he broke away and apologized.

"I'm sorry, but you're *so* fucking hot!" he claimed.

I then dusted myself off, retained my poise and grace in an instant, and acted like nothing happened. I looked at Anthony straight in the eye and said "Well, thank you. That was fun."

I never saw him again. I have not returned to that gas station since. I'll just leave him in my memory capsule. It makes me smile whenever I reminisce that encounter though. It was strange and scary but sexy in a way.

Rolling along the Paseo Padre Railroad tracks (Spring 2002)

In one of my diary entries in 2002, I wrote that "my sexual libido has reached its zenith." It was during that time when I've met numerous men and have had sexual encounters in many different places. The Paseo Padre railroad in Fremont was no exception. Behind the bushes along the railroad tracks, I got kinky with this good-looking, thirty-something guy, Holden, a couple of times.

Holden had a bad boy/punk streak. I sometimes fancy him as a Ku Klux Klan member because of his physical appearance: white as snow, steely blue eyes, shaved head, tattoos all over and a cocky demeanor. Regardless, we had a fun, kinky time. I guess my Ku Klux Klan lover was not a mean, hateful bastard after all just because he seemed to like brown pussy.

Sometime in April 2002, we agreed to meet at the El Torito restaurant parking lot along Paseo Padre Parkway in Fremont. We then proceeded to the railroad tracks not far from the restaurant, parked at the nearby residential street and walked towards the bushes.

Behind those bushes was a secret gathering spot. "Kids hang out here to drink and party and do all kinds of shit," Holden said. I myself was surprised to discover this hidden spot which reminded me of a scene from the movie *Secret Garden*. It was filled with trash though—most likely remnants of the drinking and debauchery that had taken place previously.

Instantly, I was turned on. "Oh the things I could do here," I whispered to myself.

But Holden was already thinking of the same *thing*. Without further ado, we started doing the nasty. Resting his right leg on top of a rotting tree log and grabbing on to some branches, Holden instructed me to fuck his pinkish asshole with an empty beer bottle. He knew I enjoyed doing it because we've discussed about it from our previous e-mail exchange. He also knew I loved masturbating while a guy is teasing me with his private parts; and that he did afterwards.

I was in a state of euphoria after I reached orgasm. The very thought of doing some nasty stuff in such a secluded place turned me on a great deal. I fancied myself as a runaway slut being lured into a secret hideaway by a stranger and asked to perform kinky oral sex on him. No doubt, Holden was the perfect guy to give me such treatment.

After one more enjoyable encounter of the same nature the following month, I never heard back from Holden again. I assumed it was just another spur-of-the-moment thing on the guy's part; or maybe he got lost in the bushes; or maybe my Ku Klux Klan lover decided to march his sexy white ass somewhere.

A Handsome Son of Adam at Garden City (Summer 2002)

Princess Aurora was kissed by the handsome Prince Phillip while the former *was* asleep. I was kissed by a handsome stranger while awake, thus witnessing a very sexy scene unfolding before my very eyes. It was utterly surprising and disarming.

I just had a very relaxing time with my former Latin lover, Steve, at the Grand Central Spas in San Jose that afternoon and was on my way home when all of a sudden, this tall and handsome blue eyed hunk of a man in his thirties approached me, stood near my car and without a word, made out with me.

I couldn't blame him for his bravado. He probably couldn't control his urges upon seeing me in my aquamarine halter top, short black mini skirt and high heels.

During that time period in my colorful life, I was at my *hottest*: natural golden brown complexion, straight long brown hair, a much slimmer figure, a protruding behind and legs to-die-for. During those wickedly fun times, men were dropping their pants off for me nonstop like slot machine addicts dropping coins at Cache Creek Casino. I've dated so many of them that I lost track of their names. I guess I was a walking slut machine after all with the sign "Just keep putting it in!"

But, of course, I had oozing sex appeal!

Let's go back to my very own fairy tale-like episode. After the kiss, my handsome prince simply walked away as discreetly as he had approached me, never uttering a single word.

Mixed emotions enveloped me as soon as it was over. I was surprised, shocked, shaken, turned on and flattered. "The world is really a crazy place" I told myself before driving away.

Sometimes I think of myself as a sexy fisherman (with a tinge of humor). As I sail through the uncertain seas of life, different kinds of fish and sea creatures hurl themselves on my net; fish of different sizes, shape and color, wanting to be *consumed* by me. I find it exciting though.

My "tranny" life is quite an adventure. I find myself smiling whenever I recall these bizarre incidents and sexual encounters. Dark as they may seem sometimes, for some strange reason they bring a different kind of light and luster to my life.

CHAPTER FOURTEEN

What Men Want

Although I didn't really get to know the dozens of men I've dated completely—what they were really thinking during the times we were together or what were they really like during those times when we were *not* together—I have come up with the theoretical conclusion that men will *love* you if you are able to offer them these two most important things: good conversation and a great blowjob. At least that's the case with me.

You fall short with one of these "requirements" and he will stray away and crave the mouth and tongue of another willing lover. He will then lose interest in you, sexually, and will eventually become cold and indifferent towards you. Then, as we all know it, divorce would be inevitable.

Learn to suck his cock good! It's really good for the relationship.

It will save your marriage!

Now, I don't want you to believe this theory of mine, rather I'd want you to practice it! Take some action! Tonight, after you finish reading this chapter and before you go to bed with him, take a moment, look him straight in the eye with all sincerity and sensuality, go down on him, and for heaven's sake, try your best to deep throat that *thing*! Use your tongue and slobber all over it! Multitask if you have to! Caress his balls! Play with his asshole! Do what NAPA Auto Parts does: Go the extra mile!

And when you're done, caress his chest, tummy and thighs with your fingertips. Yes, give him the feathery touch. Kiss his biceps and shoulders gently. Ask him how he's feeling. This is his "afterglow" moment. Make him bask on it. Help him savor it. You will send him to work the next morning smiling and feeling good.

It is ironic how your man, husband and boyfriend have *loved* me and appreciated me over the years, showered me with gifts and money, and yet here I am giving you sage advice on how to *keep* him. For free. That is the inner beauty of Kiki. I share. I am not the selfish type. I have a good, caring heart, too, and you can take that to the bank!

I am not only here to share my story, I am also here to save your relationships . . . and you don't have to pay for some OTC magazine with some 'been-there-done-that' sex advice. Excuse me! Please remember you are reading a fabulous book by Kiki Malachite.

My words are golden, and so *is* my tongue.

CHAPTER FIFTEEN

Nasty Girl

You hear other people say "I don't take shit from nobody!" or "I don't take crap from anyone!" Well, I know another T-girl who does, literally.

This is probably the *stinker* in this book. Thanks to my tall and handsome lover, Rob Zerano. He'll make one's dirtiest and wildest fantasy come true, regardless how nasty. He once bragged that another T-girl ate his man-dung.

He once asked me to eat his shit but for health and sanitary reasons, I declined. No human being in their right mind would oblige to such humiliation and degradation. It's absolutely *animalique*! Only rats and other foul creatures engage in such acts. I wouldn't go that *far*.

The T-girl Rob was talking about was Caraya Felixto of Hayward, CA. I used to see this girl's prostitution ads on a popular website back in the days. She claims she's a model and all that, but Rob tells me a very different story about her.

Rob said Caraya liked sniffing his butthole and inhaling the farts he would release.

After some minutes of sniffing, Caraya would then lie on her back and have Rob shoot shit down her face. If some turd misses her eager mouth, Caraya would then push the human droppings close to her mouth with her very own fingers and eat them.

Rob also told me that there was even one occasion sometime in the summer of 2008 when he brought with him another guy to join in the "poop-a-thon". "It was a very nasty threesome," Rob detailed. "Caraya's face was unrecognizable after we were done."

Rob said Caraya looked liked a public toilet bowl that had not been cleaned for days after that session.

I guess most of you are wondering what my point is in sharing this revolting story. Well, I outright denounce hypocrisy and despise those who practice it. I am no saint, but definitely a sinner. I am 100% honest about it and I speak my mind.

I have personally seen and read the prostitution ads that human toilet would post on the internet. She would even badmouth other *trans-titutes*; claiming she's the best looking, et cetera, et cetera. It's a shame that she had the balls to self-promote, when there is a second party telling a very different story about her and her sordid acts.

I guess Caraya was full of shit after all, literally and figuratively. No wonder I enjoy bashing hypocrites like her online with my too-hot-to-handle blogs and online posts. I simply have to speak my mind.

On my part, I only have this to say about my sexual skills. I may not eat a man's shit but I know damn well how to *eat* him. I also know that there are people out there who are willing to suffice my claims if necessary: that if there is only one quintessential lover around—a transsexual Casanova—I believe that person is me. Bar none. I am the ultimate sex lioness, *not* a kitten. But for a lioness, I am ten times powerful. I can make the most masculine man around moan as if he were having a thousand orgasms. I can make his steely, strong body shake and shiver with my butterfly touch. I can make his toes curl from the out-of-this-world pleasure my eager tongue gives. I can bring excitement and erotica back to his life starting with my wet, warm kisses. I can make all his fantasies come true. I am Kiki Malachite, and I am to be *cherished!* Yes, I demand that, god damn it! I am one of the greatest sexual beings ever to walk the face of the earth.

CHAPTER SIXTEEN

One Classy Lady

I believe I am one classy lady. After reading all those heartwarming e-mail, letters and text messages I have received over the years from friends, lovers and relatives, not to mention the compliments I have gotten from strangers, I suppose I am, after all, one real classy lady. I suppose it is in-born, too. It's in my blood. I came from a well-respected clan. The vintage family portrait (taken in the 1950s) on display in my living room that shows my paternal grandfather with his grandmother, aunts and uncles, is one of my greatest inspirations. My grandfather's aunts were some of the classiest women in the family; even in old age. I am proud and happy to have met them all when I was a young teen. They were already in their eighties at the time. In that family portrait, one would find these fabulous women wearing big cocktail rings and the chicest dresses from the Retro period.

Naturally, I play the part. I carry myself well in public. It surprises me when cashiers, waiters, DMV agents, store clerks and bank tellers treat me nicely than others while at their place of business. Of course, I know there are some raised eyebrows whenever that happens. I just smile devilishly like Glenn Close from *Dangerous Liasons* and whisper "Loser."

Some people tell me I have the demeanor and deportment of an aristocratic person. I am not rich or wealthy though. But I am rich with `elan, great ideas and common sense.

Well, back to that "demeanor" shit. I should know better. Of course, I do! An elegant demeanor takes you a long way and a simple but sincere smile will seal the deal. Show people that you respect yourself and they will show you respect in return. You earn respect. You do *not* expect it. It's another powerful principle of mine.

The only drawback with looking rich and fabulous is that . . . good-looking bums and sexy boytoys tend to have a field day with me. It's fun though. I like it when they approach me, give me those silly pick up lines and flirt with me. I relish the thought of being *satisfied* by a handsome but penniless young man `*a la* Brian Waxberg; while wearing my diamonds and pearls; smoking cigarettes and drinking wine. Not to mention putting some Godiva candies between his pretty but impoverished lips. Oh, what decadence!

Well, let's go back to looking good and being dressed to the nines. Of course, you cannot please everybody. Sometimes no matter how dignified and elegant you look, rude and disrespectful people will always be rude and disrespectful. Whenever I find myself in such situations, I naturally give them a dose of their own medicine; or maybe worse. Honey, I didn't spend two hours making myself look this beautiful and I didn't spend thousands of dollars on my fine, solid gold jewelry only to get disrespected! Walk away or bow down, bitch!

In the early years of my transgender-hood, the circumstances for me were bad. I succumbed to bad influence and advice. I was tempted by the demons and became their whore. I made bad decisions in life. I was young and stupid. It's a cliché, but it is so true.

But alas, there is light at the end of the tunnel. I guess I've finally reached it. And no, I'm not talking about the Caldecott Tunnel, god damn it! I am talking about the tunnel of life that leads to success and other wonderful things.

It's 2011 now and things are very different for me. I make wise decisions these days and I continue to chase my dreams. Well, I still chase asses occasionally, but, that's another story. I am more focused than before when it comes to achieving my goals. I guess I owe this newfound emotional stability to my own concrete determination. I realized I have to make my life better.

I love reading and learning. Even when I was plastered and felt beaten after a late night *sexcapade* during my wild days, I found and made time to read.

I love reading about royalty and grand, fabulous things. I enjoy reading books by or about Beaton, Vreeland, Von Furstenberg, Avedon, Chanel, and Schiaparelli. They are my "personal bibles".

I also enjoy watching TCM movies that feature the most stylish women of Hollywood's Golden Age and their graceful, dignified moves; Vivien Leigh, Grace Kelly, Deborah Kerr, Lauren Bacall, Joan Crawford and Lana Turner to name a few.

Whenever I execute natural grace and perfect deportment, and apply the things I learned from these style icons, the outcome is always bedazzling.

I know we all live our lives a certain way, but if we add style and pizzazz to it, good things will follow.

Good, positive attitude is a key ingredient. Take your work seriously but also learn to have fun like it's the end of the world! That's what I call a "perfect balance."

Communication skills are very important and therefore should be given much attention. I always tell friends and family that talking to people is itself a form of art. First, you have to have good attitude. Second, smile. Third, don't be boring. Listen to what the other person has to say first then respond with your own views and opinion. While you're at it, interject some humor or a funny anecdote that might be of relation to the topic which both of you are discussing. Humor tends to lighten up serious, dry conversations.

Image is *everything*. If you want people to take you seriously, put on some serious clothes and jewelry. A well-dressed individual represents success and class.

People become interested and fascinated. One thing though, cut down on fake or costume jewelry. Sometimes they make a person look like a "try hard" or maybe even struggling. Remember, the look of *money* is the look of everything! And what better way to make a statement than to adorn oneself with fabulous gold and diamond jewelry.

Also, remember that what looks good on those Nordstrom and Macy's models doesn't necessarily look good on you. Put on some clothes that are classy and timeless, and pair them with pearl earrings or diamond studs; a wide gold bracelet or a dainty necklace. A big gemstone ring is also essential. I find it more fun and useful than a regular diamond ring. Most of the time, people would grab my hand and admire the cocktail ring I am wearing at the moment. When it comes to a diamond ring, unless you don't mind breaking the bank on a cluster ring that has colorless or near-colorless stones, go for it. Remember, rhinestones are for cowboys and genuine, sparkling diamonds are for real ladies.

I always feel I'm on top of the world when I adorn my body with solid gold jewelry. That feeling is priceless! I go by the saying "Only gold is treasured." Plus, I have sensitive skin. I can't stand mystery metals or gold-plated jewelry rubbing on my skin.

A subtle scent of fragrance helps, too. A dab here and there of Chanel 5 or Fendi Palazzo won't hurt. A good smelling person is an attractive person. Also, you are sure to create a lasting impression.

I can never recall the many times friends and acquaintances have commented on how good I smell whenever I grace their parties and special events. It gets funny to a point sometimes, but it is absolutely flattering. Some of my all-time favorite fragrances include *Lolita Lempicka*, Clinique *Happy* and J.Lo's *Miami Glow*.

CHAPTER SEVENTEEN

Cherishing Life

I am now laying low from living a debauched life *a` la* Marquis de Sade. I am staying home more and spending more quality time with my loved ones instead of my lovers. I still have time for my *studs*, don't get me wrong, but not as much. I enjoy wearing my 18 karat gold dangling earrings these days and the days of hard, hot, kinky sex seem to be slowly evading me.

I revel under the sun more than at night. These days, I am more focused on having afternoon tea in my spacious backyard; on tedious yet therapeutic hobbies such as scrapbooking and photo-organizing; on rummaging the contents of second-hand and antique stores in search of vintage, one-of-a-kind pieces; on sitting on the green grass at the park, savoring the fresh air rather than the musky, manly odor of my battalion of lovers. I try to stay outdoors more these days, rather than indoors; far more different than when I used to stay inside my dark and dreary hotel room for hours.

At night, I enjoy reading and re-reading some of my favorite books—mostly memoirs—while having hot tea, sliced fruits and a Milky Way or Snickers candy bar; or maybe a slice of cake. I also find reruns of *Murder, She Wrote, The Golden Girls* and *The Nanny* fun to watch. Don't ask me how I've memorized the lines of the last two shows' theme songs.

I am living and loving life better these days. I eat healthier now and am using Hershey's syrup on my banana split rather than my lovers' *bananas*. Well, I am still open to the idea. These days, I'm eating the real white meat more, instead of the o*ther* white meat hanging between the thighs of the many Johns, Jims and Mikes I know.

I treat my body now as a Nutritionist's refrigerator rather than Mr. Notrevenko's personal trash bin (Oh, those big Russian studs!). I just want to *put* the good, fresh and healthy stuff in it. The nasty ideas still make me giggle, but at this point, I'd like to change my ways. Change for better health and living. Well, wish me luck! My young Irish lover, John Calwein, just sent me an e-mail, asking me when we'll be able to have some *fun* again . . . and some *Jack Daniels*.

One thing that attracts my fancy more these days is collecting vintage and Estate jewelry.

I just love my jewelry collection. I am so crazy over it. When I look at each piece, I see my hard work and success. You feel much prouder when you know you've worked hard for—and paid for—your own jewelry instead of inheriting them from your parents or grandparents. They have more meaning. At least that's how I feel about it.

I'm so crazy about my gold and diamond jewelry, as well as the other precious pieces I possess. Most of them are one-of-a-kind pieces, purchased from Estate auctions, fabulous jewelry stores on Rodeo Drive and antiques stores all over the country. I am so proud to have them. I tell you, it takes a connoisseur's eye to acquire such rare, beautiful pieces, and I just love flaunting them. I don't buy new jewelry because the new ones are boring and have less gold content. I want more *bang* for my buck! Plus, I wouldn't be caught dead wearing the same piece of jewelry that another person has.

Also, I'm wearing my jewelry more these days—my fabulous and expensive jewelry—not while getting fucked and violated, but rather while treating the mall promenade, numerous city downtowns and trendy streets with a cosmopolitan vibe, as my personal fashion runways.

You should see my fabulous 18 karat gold bracelet collection. They don't make those sizes anymore. They are big, bold and solid gold! I am so proud of them. Seriously!

Oh, and by the way. Have you seen my 21 carat Swiss blue topaz ring? I know, I just can't stop blabbing about it. How about my fabulous shield style gold and Lapis Lazuli ring and Art Deco era onyx and diamond cocktail ring? And let's not forget about my fantastic dome enamel ring with droplets of diamonds, sapphires, rubies and emeralds. How about my vintage two inches long, 4 carat cabochon Ruby ring by *Virgilio*? How about my 22 karat solid gold marquis shape ring that is over an inch long? I must warn you—these pieces might make Duchess of Windsor green with envy in her grave. My recent purchase was this humongous 40 plus carats Lemon Quartz ring set in gold. F-A-B-U-L-O-U-S!

Other outstanding pieces from my collection that I love so much include a rare Chopard pocket watch by Tiffany & Co. in solid 18 karat gold. Also in my possession is a gigantic emerald cocktail ring. I also love my vintage Chanel earrings. Fabulous! They are all fabulous!

I've said this before and I will say it again: I love the attention! I bask on the endless stares and whispers my mall and restaurant trips generate. I could never recall the number of times I've received flattering and heartwarming comments because of the fabulous jewelry I wear. I don't have to be a celebrity because I know I am already one in my own right. And, naturally, I make the world my stage.

At San Jose's Valley Fair Mall in December 2008, I wore my stunning 4-carat diamond cluster ring with sparkling round and baguette near colorless stones. It overpowered my power finger as well as the senses of the four employees at the four different jewelry stores I visited that day. Those men and women were absolutely captivated! They seemed more proud and happy than me. They should be. Fabulous ladies like me with an equally fabulous jewelry collection are hard to find these days.

And when I say *fabulous* I meant to include execution of grace and deportment, class and personality. I've seen many broads wear nice clothes and jewelry (i.e. some women of *The Real Housewives* series), but the minute they open their mouth, get into catfights and just basically show a lack of respect for others and themselves, I just shake my head. Pathetic!

I give most of them the "Commodus thumbs down". Yes, you remember that scene from *Gladiator*, right?

Your jewelry *must* match your demeanor and deportment. You can't be wearing a five thousand dollar diamond ring and be acting like a five dollar street whore. It just doesn't connect. It's stupid!

I believe I am one of the last few women alive who knows how to combine grace, class, personality and fabulous jewelry.

I just love showing off my fabulous jewelry collection and the rest of my fine little treasures. Cortes himself would be hunting me down over them if he's still alive.

I could never recall the many times people have stopped me to give me compliments for the fabulous jewelry that I'm wearing. It's insane! I believe a true lady should wear her jewelry all the time. You do not keep them in a safe somewhere! That's silly!

I will wear mine till they fall out of my neck, wrists and fingers!

"Treasures of pleasure" is how I call them. It's a favorite quote of mine. When I make people happy and see them smiling because of the nice things I possess, my feet lift up from the ground. I am in heaven. It's an understated validation of how high and fabulous my tastes are. Kate from Briarwood Antiques in Downtown San Jose once told me, "You have good eye!"

And, of course, for the benefit of good karma—always—I thank the masses for the praises.

CHAPTER EIGHTEEN

Comments, Criticisms and Observations

The world is definitely full of dark, delightful and disdainful characters. Here's my take on some of them.

1) Sarah Palin's head is so full of shit. No wonder that ridiculous hair continues to pile up!

2) On Bristol Palin's obvious plastic surgery and other antics: It's her own way of giving people a distraction because she knows damn well the public is so sick and tired of the older Palin's stupidity and publicity stunts.

3) George W. Bush, Scooter Libby, Dick Cheney, Karl Rove, and Donald Rumsfeld should be the ones in Guantanamo Bay.

4) Anyone can be fabulous. It really depends on how you look at yourself and your level of self esteem. Be creative. Go to vintage stores! Get yourself a fabulous vintage blouse and a big cocktail ring and most importantly, *act* and feel fabulous! You don't have to be a celebrity to feel like one.

5) Always remember . . .

   a) Celebrities and yourself fart out the same farts and poop the same poop, so please don't feel like they are better or superior than you!

   b) Be original. Be yourself!

c) The world is your oyster and you are a beautiful pearl. Let the world discover your inner beauty by contributing for its betterment and doing good things to others.

d) Don't be a "Hollywood celebrity" follower. The term "Hollywood" is just a fantasy, an illusion. Some of those "Hollywood" celebrities are deviants and drug addicts anyway; absolutely not the role models you're looking for.

e) To some teenage girls: Never compare or liken yourself with trashy and trampy reality TV "celebrities." All you're going to learn from them is tackiness, stupidity and bad make up.

f) Work hard for your future and reputation. Only you can make a name for yourself. Only you can create your own legacy.

6) Please use Facebook as an online tool for connecting with old friends and relatives; not for posting the same old tired haggard photos of yourself round the clock and talking about your boring, mediocre life. And please don't make up stuff about yourself just to build an image! You're fooling no one except you.

7) To the TV stations that continuously produce shows about dating and "finding" the right partner: Please! We don't need to see who that Bachelor or Bachelorette is going to fuck next time! These people *are* dogs. Obviously, these losers have a ton-load of insecurities in them. They have to go on national TV for attention and try to fool others by pretending to be somebody that they're not.

8) One question I have for these so-called "Hollywood celebrities" we see on TV today: What good have you done for the poor and the sick lately?

9) Two thumbs up and a bunch of "Thank You" shout outs to Oprah Winfrey, Brad Pitt, Angelina Jolie, George Clooney, Elton John, Bono and Elizabeth Taylor for their concern and contribution to society.

10) I once had a discussion with a friend about prostitutes, *brostitutes* and other whores. He asked my opinion about the matter. My response was: "Actually, in every business and building, there is a whore. He or she will do *anything* and anyone in the company just to get promoted and get a better position. Whores and hustlers are not necessarily found on the streets."

11) Some Filipinos have a penchant for singing the Sinatra standard "My Way" at parties and karaoke bars. Please! Sing it only if you've *really* accomplished something major in your life!

12) Where to spot rude, tacky and uncouth "celebrities": at awards shows. Some of them don't applaud when their competition wins; some of them are caught making faces and some do not show respect by giving a standing ovation to a performer or honoree (when the rest of the audience rises). So tacky! Thank god for the zoom crew! It's like having a bird's eye view of the audience.

13) How to spot an insecure woman: when she sees a good-looking, classy lady and immediately becomes "clingy" to her boyfriend or husband (i.e. holding on to his hand tightly all of a sudden and constantly trying to get his attention or kissing him nonstop). Pathetic!

14) Always say "No!" to drama queens. It's 2011 and that's the last thing we need. If you have some problems with your family, friend or husband, get over it! Make peace! Soldier on! Life is not perfect so stop acting like a victim all the time! More importantly, don't take it on other people who do not have the slightest clue on what's going on with your life.

15) Loud moans and groans from sluts, skanks and whores at hotels is one of my pet peeves. I wish someone would stuff these bitches' mouths with men's used socks and used toilet paper while getting fucked.

16) My most sincere message to bitches who give me the look just because I look drop dead gorgeous every time I walk in an establishment, looking chic and classy with my fine jewelry and fabulous handbags, and carrying myself with an aristocratic deportment: "Go fuck yourself! With a rusty metal bar!"

17) Does the phrase "Tie the knot" really mean "to get married"? I think it should be rephrased into "tie the nut." Men, be careful. Once you get married you're going to have a hard time escaping. Being married is not like going inside a candy store wherein you *taste* different things enjoyably and leave at your own free will when you're done. Oh no, no, no! You taste it, you keep it, my friend! So, think about the consequences of "tying the knot" a thousand times before you tie yourself up with that crazy bitch.

18) The only valid reason why some guys join that "reality" show about a bachelorette is to get laid. Plain and simple. They're not really after a serious relationship; just a serious lay. *Puh-leeze!* Give me a break!

19) Gold-diggers are no different than the filthiest whores around. They just wear better clothes.

20) I recently viewed some Facebook profiles of people I know and all I can say to them is: "Get a life! Your lives are boring!" I mean, who posts stuff about being at a department store or doing a simple, everyday task?

21) A message to some Republi*cunts* who have a penchant for using arguments such as same sex marriage and gay and immigration rights as forefronts to their atrocious and misleading election (and re-election) campaign strategies: "Just fuck off and fuck each other! Your party is overflowing with perverts, hypocrites and imbeciles anyway!"

22) To some of my relatives and former acquaintances in the Philippines who still can't get over the fact that I have become a successful person here in the US and that I am currently reaping the benefits of my hard work, I hope you change your ugly ways and that one day you'll cease to have that kind of negative attitude.

23) A message to someone I know with a questionable character: "Did you marry that guy because you love him or because you love the kind of lifestyle he's giving you?"

24) Whoever coined the term 'revenge look' must be guillotined. No one's telling you to dress like a five dollar street whore just to spite and insult your ex-boyfriend or ex-husband. When a guy's through with you, he could care less. Even if you fuck all the animals in the farm nearby.

25) A bi-curious male friend of mine once asked me about *trans*-titutes near *Divas* in San Francisco. He was hoping to meet someone who looks like Marilyn Monroe. All I could tell him was "Good luck! I hope you don't end up with a Marlon Brando."

26) Recently, Kate Middleton's sister, Pippa, created headlines when a photograph of her on the passenger side of a convertible, along with three men—presumably her gangbang squad—surfaced in the media. In it, one of her male friends is seen toting a handgun and is more than likely taunting the person who's taking the picture. First of all, I just hope they end up shooting at each other instead of

harming the innocent public, and secondly, contrary to what others say that Pippa is "pretty" or even "good-looking," I really think she's the skinnier version—with a tan—of comedian/actress Caroline Rhea. I have respect for Caroline Rhea because she *has* talent. As for Pippa, The Church of England—even Westminster Abbey—won't be able to save her from my initial impression of her: just another twat with a tan. No further comment.

27) I suppose after hearing about the not-so-secret services rendered by those Colombian whores to President Obama's Secret Service entourage, Joes and Johns should really be more cautious when hooking up with trashier-than-trash hookers. No pun intended.

28) Within my family circle, I really believe my four beautiful sisters set the standard when it comes to how to properly apply the right amount of make up and how to dress in a cool and chic manner. Nowadays, I see a good lot of my female relations and family friends desperately try to look like my gorgeous siblings; but to no avail, unfortunately.

CHAPTER NINETEEN

Favorite Things, Random Thoughts & Cherished Expressions

Kiki Malachite's every day life would not be complete and exciting without a carousel of dark and colorful thoughts and jabs coming from her ever acerbic tongue. She also includes a potpourri of her favorite things.

1) "Carry on!"
2) Some alternate titles for *James Bond 007* movies by Kiki: *Diamonds are for my Lover, Moonrimmer, You Only Lick Twice, Otto's Pussy (Oh, those Euro guys!), GoldenBrownEye, For Your Ass Only*
3) "I'll kick your ass so hard you'll end up back in the province where you came from, bitch!" (My favorite expression when having a verbal spat with a mean Filipino here in the US)
4) "Shut your faggot ass up!" (Yelled out this obscenity several times during a 2006 verbal spat with another driver along Mathilda Avenue in Sunnyvale, CA)
5) "I'll kick your ass so hard you'll end up back in your mother's hairy pussy!"
6) "Ten dollars, you say?" (2010: My excited response to a jeweler offering me discounts on some silver rings with genuine gemstones; he meant to say "One hundred ten," but I didn't hear him well)
7) "You're such a bad boy" (My favorite response to the *sext* messages I receive from my young lovers)

8) "Make me a happy woman today" (When summoning a lover in his late 30s or early 40s to *do* me; they're the best!)

9) "I skipped school today, Daddy" (My favorite line when role-playing with an older lover)

10) I love it when I blow cigarette smoke on my lover's face while he is pleasing me.

11) I once challenged a man to get back to the parking lot so I could beat him up after he yelled out obscenities at me outside the Keypoint building along Mathilda Avenue in Sunnyvale, CA. The drunkard pretended he didn't hear me and just drove away. Gentlemen, that's what I call *a* big, fat old pussy! They can still meow but they run away when you go after them.

12) Trevor Reedley of San Francisco is one of the genuine "bad boys" I've met: a dirty blond-haired Jamba Juice employee by day and a hustler at night; with ear piercing and tattoos. Yummy!

13) I love eating food with lots of onion and garlic before having sex. It just boosts my sex drive *to* six speed and launches my libido as high as the International Space Station. I always have a bottle of Listerine handy though.

14) I really love my red BCBG bag, vintage gold amethyst ring, 1940s 18 karat wide gold bracelet and 24 karat Credit Suisse pendant necklace—purchases from The Junior League of SF Next-to-New store many years ago. Some of my all-time favorite possessions!

15) I simply despise inattentive, stupid and reckless drivers especially if they drive luxury cars like Mercedes Benzes and Jaguars. Makes me think they are scullery maids and unlicensed idiots who snuck those cars out of their bosses' garage for a joyride. I don't care if you're driving the most expensive car in the world. If you can't follow simple traffic rules and have no respect for other drivers, please go home and eat rat poison.

16) Things I'd flat out say to road jerks who like to cut other drivers and pull crazy stunts on the road (if we ever end up in the same destination): "You're such an asshole like your mother!" and "I hope you have the balls to cut me right now like what you did on the freeway, bitch!"

17) I sometimes contemplate on asking the tall and handsome Fremont, California Olive Garden waiter to get on all fours on top of my table and let me have him for dessert. I'd put a peeled banana somewhere

on top of his sexy body and top it off with Hershey's syrup, whip cream and cherries. *Delicious!*

18) I always give to the poor and homeless. If I could spend thousands of dollars on jewelry and other nice things, what is a dollar for an old man to buy food for his empty tummy?

19) I really think those TV commercials about dating sites are plain boring, unrealistic and simply corny. Love comes naturally, not through *e-Harmon . . .* well, you know what I'm talking about.

20) I'd rather spend my credit card minimum payment on a strapping young lad with a fat wad. It's a lesson I'd like to teach those inconsiderate and rude credit card company Customer Service representatives. Honestly, I don't give a rat's ass to the term "good credit." And to me, it's absolutely worth it! Why give away my forty, when I can buy my boytoy some beer and get lucky?

21) Sage words from an honest Cupertino, CA jeweler I know: "Only your health and happiness matter in this world. Everything else is a joke." I'll never forget that.

22) Wearing nice clothes and fabulous jewelry definitely command respect; especially if you carry yourself well when out in public. People treat you differently. So girls, try to look and act classy, not trashy. Always!

23) Another fashion rule: Keep the clothes chic and simple but make your jewelry and accessories stand out.

24) I think the armpits of local basketball players Brian Ames and Derek Fuchs are the most photographed in town. They're so cute. I sometimes wonder if the local newspaper photographer has an armpit addiction.

25) *Bun appétit!*—A favorite expression I say to myself before munching on my lover's sexy body parts; with a devilish grin.

26) Movies that made a great impression: *Sunset Boulevard, Summertime, How to Marry a Millionaire, Rear Window, An Affair to Remember, Designing Woman, Auntie Mame* (1958), *Butterfield 8, The Roman Spring of Mrs. Stone, Breakfast at Tiffany's, Alfie* (with Michael Caine), *Midnight Cowboy, Deliverance, Dangerous Liasons, The Affair of the Necklace, Girl with a Pearl Earring, The Count of Monte Cristo* (Jim Caviezel looks delicious!), *Gosford Park, Beowulf, Clash of the Titans* (2010), *Drive* and *The Avengers*

27) TV shows and movies that generate repulsion: Any TV show or movie that has Susan Lucci in it or an old hag fucking a young stud. Disgusting!

28) Songs that made a great impression:

Smoke Gets in Your Eyes by The Platters—I prefer versions of female artists, but regardless, this song is sexy and sentimental; so true to the heart. Love it!

Rainy Days and Mondays by The Carpenters—My number one favorite Carpenters song whenever I have my karaoke session at home. Like most people, I find Mondays dreadful; but I get over it when I sing this song.

Can't Stay Away From You by Gloria Estefan—A ballad that overflows with emotional want and infatuation that whenever I listen to it I get *lost*. Such a beautiful song!

Kiss of Life by Sade—Every day is worth living for, no matter how other people try to ruin it. Plus, I just think of a lover who gives me the best sex.

A Little Respect by Erasure—I know I can be a mean bitch sometimes, but a little respect won't hurt. Thank you!

Human by The Pretenders—I can be mean, I can be nice, I can be nasty, but most importantly, I'm just me. So, please leave the judging to God!

Here Comes the Rain Again by Eurythmics—This song reminds me of my grade school years in Manila and the back to back tropical storms that hit the Philippines from 1983 to 1984; but what stands out the most are the haunting lyrics, catchy melody and music video.

Why by Annie Lenox—A break up song that is so full of drama (I love the music video, too); the perfect song to play when you're about to throw a beer bottle at the bathroom mirror, with your mascara dripping down your face, crying buckets.

Bizarre Love Triangle (Frente! version)—Reminds me of the fun, carefree times I had back in Manila, when I'd cut classes and spend the afternoon at the mall, shopping and thumbing up the pages of countless books about the British Royal Family inside *National Bookstore*.

Prayer for the Dying by Seal—Reminds me of my last days in Manila, before flying to the US in 1994. Plus, the combination of the song's melody and Seal's chant-like vocals takes me to another dimension.

The Rose by Bette Midler—One of the dozens of songs I clearly remember that played during the one and only car ride I had with my late uncle, Tony. They were living in SF's Treasure Island at the time and he asked me to come with him to pick up his wife (who at the time was working at the Alameda Naval Air Station).

Wonderful by Adam Ant—Anthem from the heart dedicated to the friends and relatives I left in the Philippines back in 1994 to live a brand new life in the US; also reminds me of my one and only true love, Mark Aldredge.

Spiderwebs by No Doubt—Gwen Stefani was so cool back then (and she still is!)

Take a Picture by Filter—Sort of like a freeze frame of a very special moment I am having with a friend or lover.

1979 by The Smashing Pumpkins—Love its music video. I see myself doing those crazy things back in high school *if* I were that rebellious and wild. I was such a good girl though. Regardless, it's one of my favorite '90s songs.

Tonight, Tonight by The Smashing Pumpkins—This over the top stadium theme always reminds me of the summer vacation I had in sunny San Diego back in 1996; those endless freeways, watching the Atlanta Olympics, and the handsome boys of Sycuan Casino! I feel like a winner already!

Barely Breathing by Duncan Sheik—My "get-pumped-up-to-work" song back in the late '90s; while driving my '75 Super Beetle, summer wind on my face. Ah, *the* glory days of youth!

Say You'll Be There by Spice Girls—A message to my lovers: Please be there when I summon you.

Tubthumping by Chumbawamba—Another "get-pumped-up-to-work" song.

Hit Me with your Best Shot by Pat Benatar—One of my favorite karaoke songs.

I Like Big Butts by Sir Mix A Lot—I simply like big (male) butts.

And the other songs that get me excited when meeting my male friends and lovers are . . . *Call Me* by Blondie, *Private Dancer* by Tina Turner, *Glamorous Life* by Sheila E, *Material Girl* by Madonna, *Stir it Up* by Patti LaBelle, *Wild Women Do* by Natalie Cole, and *Money Changes Everything* by Cyndi Lauper.

29) Maximo di Simonti of San Francisco is a total jerk! I still haven't forgotten that one night in January 2002 when this asshole walked out on me outside *Boulevard* restaurant by the Embarcadero.
30) If I were a photographer, I would entice my client to smile by shouting out the lines "Smile! Smile! Yes, give me big smiles! Smile like you just saw the biggest cock in the world!"
31) Some botox*ed* rich bitch in Florida decided to leave most of her money to her pet chihuahua. It was in the news back in June 2010. First of all, I think she's crazy and secondly, she just wants attention. Proof that no amount of botox and make up can get you all the attention you desire. You really have to do something stupid first!
32) 5 Types of People on my Blacklist

The Spider type

The type of person who shows up at a party and would start weaving tales and stories of self-promotion; so that others would become interested and start gathering around him or her and . . . voila! The guests got entangled . . . with lies. Narcissists, go to hell!

A Person with the "Bilbo Baggins Complex"

The type of person who's having a hard time letting go of a position even though the entire world is telling him or her it's time to go. Majority wins, please. It's high time that you lower the pride flag!

The Café Bull-e' type

A pretentious type of person or group of people who *demands* being seated outside small cafes and restaurants, acting as if they're minding their own business but actually checking out my Louis Vuitton Murakami Multi-color bag, fabulous jewelry and chic and classy demeanor. Sad to say, but my most favorite city in California—Mountain View—and Fillmore Street in San Francisco are infested with these kinds of people especially on weekends.

The Beggar of Beverly Hills

A good friend of mine from L.A. once complained about her ambitious neighbor named Bella who's a bit of a *cuckoo*, too; who moved to Los Angeles from the Philippines about ten years ago to pursue a "singing career." Well, her visa expired and so did her dreams. She decided to remain in the US illegally and started a family—pressuring her disfigured husband to impregnate her twice so when the little tykes grow up and turn eighteen, one of them could legally petition her, making her eligible to apply for a Green Card. It's a long, complicated story. Immigration Law Offices of Los Angeles would best explain it. At any rate, my friend has always treated her like a *bona fide* bum of Beverly Hills. She likes hanging out in the area even though she hasn't got a single penny for shopping. She continually posts messages on her Facebook account about the small adventures she and her poor little boys have in BH (i.e. a trip to McDonalds). Pathetic! The best advice I would give this vagrant is do what General MacArthur did: return to the Philippines!

The Hoochie mama

I know their fashion sense and perception about themselves are twisted, but for further cautionary (and sanitary) measures, I make sure I spray some Lysol when they're around.

The Knocked up Whore

These knocked up skanks would intentionally block department store aisles with baby walkers and carriers, thinking the world should put up with their crap and be sympathetic to them in general. I'm just glad I *make* every aisle my red carpet no matter what, so try as they might, these losers will never have their way; at least while I'm within their parameter. I make it a habit to push their baby strollers (a.k.a. welfare ticket) to the side. These walking vultures would have to fuck a bunch of bums first, get their ugly bellies ballooning again, eat a ton of pickles and shit out a bunch of unruly creatures before they could make me raise an eye brow. At the end of the day, I just tell myself "Be happy you're not a streetwalker and a welfare whore like them!" These despicable creatures would suck Uncle Sam's asshole if that's the only way to get money from him!

33) Sex articles by *Cosmopolitan* and *Glamour* magazines are written for virgins, novices and women who are *really* bad in bed. (And I mean "bad" as in poor-performing)

34) *Cougwhores*: Older broads who are on the prowl for younger *cubs* to further announce their insecurities and dissatisfaction in life. I think these people are disgusting. Gloria Steinem better give them a beating. I've seen some in public and honestly, they are not the nicest people around (bad make up, bad fashion, and terrible attitude).

35) I'll be sure to use the Bible as reference when the time comes that I become senile and eventually forget the names of the many men I've dated. God bless all the Johns, Lukes and Marks, and all those good-looking sons of Adam!

36) I think the James Bond .007 flick *From Russia with Love* has the most homoerotic scenes you could find in a so-called "macho" movie. I simply love it! In there you will find the blond Russian villain forcing Sean Connery to kiss his foot (S&M, maybe?).

Another scene features James Bond yanking the Russian villain's suit (Prelude to mad, passionate love-making?); and perhaps the kinkiest scene of them all was when James Bond "gassed" the villain using his attache` case (Domination and humiliation?). It may not be in the screenplay writer's subconscious, but ironically, the innuendos are hard to miss for someone like myself who is familiar with such sexual proclivities.

37) I also think *Lord of the Rings: The Fellowship of the Ring* Part 1 has some amusing gay lines. Note the part when Aragorn, Legalos and Gimli pledge their support for Frodo: Aragorn with the line "You have my *sword*"; Legalos with the line "You have my *bow*" (sound is similar to "balls"); and Gimli with the line "You have my *ax*" (sound is similar to "ass" or "arse").

38) A perfect and peaceful day for me at home includes hearing my beautiful two year-old niece sing along with kiddie songs on TV and the internet; myself listening to songs of Ella, Sarah Vaughan and Barbra; having a hot cup of Swiss Miss cocoa drink and reminiscing the wonderful times I had with long gone lovers and other people that matter. I'd lie down, close my eyes and start gathering those sweet memories over and over. Ah, what peace and happiness!

39) A great way for me to feel recharged with utter fabulousness is by thumbing up the pages of the book *QUEEN ELIZABETH The Queen Mother* by Godfrey Talbot. I can't get enough of this great lady's jewelry, handbags, charm and grace!

40) The three greatest pleasures in life are kinky sex, great food and having lots of money.

41) Don't forget to say a little prayer of thanks every day.

42) Don't cut people on the road just because you're driving a BMW or riding a racing motorcycle. The world is not impressed if you're driving a BMW or riding a Ducati. It really puts a smile on my face when these road rats get cut off by another driver. Bad karma has a strange way of avenging responsible drivers like me. And please stop acting like you're a NASCAR driver because you're not and you'll never be! Even if your crazy mother promised you!

43) Comedienne Kathy Griffin is my number one favorite. She's very funny, she's a natural, she's painfully honest and she will always be an A-List celebrity to me.

44) Reward yourself every time you accomplish something, whether it's big or small. Life is too short. Treat yourself to some cheeseburger, fries, milk shake and cheese cake! Or a beautiful piece of jewelry!

45) Some of the most memorable drives I made happened during my numerous trips to Salinas back in 2004 (along highway 101 near Watsonville) and to Santa Cruz (along Highway 17; through the zigzag part of that highway wherein all you see ahead of you are the majestic hills that seem to open up as you pass through). It reminds me of a scene from Fairy Tale Theater's *The Pied Piper of Hamelin.* Oh, how beautiful California truly is!

46) If ever I decide to acquire a pet pig, I'd name it "Sutafel."

47) To the naysayers and some hypocritical relatives (yes, sad but true) out there who came up with the verdict stating that I won't make it just because: Dream on! Why not write a book instead of writing lies and looking for dirty pussy on the internet? I curse you to live in envy and discontent for as long as you see me around. I smile each time you frown at me and say bad things behind my back. God *is* the only judge!

48) I greatly admire Bill Maher and Anderson Cooper for hosting shows that are filled with straightforward commentaries and no holds barred criticisms. These men really *have* balls!

49) If I were to make a short film I'd give it the title *Baby Semaji, Yorg is Your Real Father!*

50) For me, the sexiest body parts of a man are his butt cheeks, jaw line and biceps.

51) My bedroom acrobatics would surely put the techniques of those *Cirque du Soleil* performers to shame.

52) My nosy bum of a neighbor, Kevrin Boils—a total disgrace to humanity—is the most despicable creature ever to walk the face of the earth. Unemployed for almost two decades (I better do a background check one of these days), this sinister creature has progressively made a career out of minding other people's business over the years. Fat, short and ugly, my favorite nickname for this scum of the earth is . . . well, "fat, old, bitch."

53) Sometimes I fancy myself as a transvestite pirate: I always have eye make up on, I wear rings all the time and I'm always looking for *booty*!

54) Antonio, a handsome Yahoo Messenger "chat mate" from Italy in the early 2000s recently reconnected with me online. All I could tell him was "I'd like to see you and your friend Matteo bend over again and shake your sexy soccer player asses in front of the webcam." Hot, hot, hot!

55) The three handsomest male models on the internet today are Pavel Novotny, Jakub Stefano and Matus Valent.

56) Watching the handsome and smooth Gino (my one-time lover from Turkey) sleep in deep slumber—and in the nude—was one of the greatest sexual turn ons I've ever experienced (December 2005). The scene reminded me of a Greek Mythology story wherein Psyche was described gazing at the sleeping Cupid. So erotic!

57) I recently saw profiles of former boytoys Jamie K, Georgie M and Gleb B on Facebook and couldn't help coming up with these sexy anecdotes: the ice cold bottle of Pepsi that I gave to then-struggling college student Jamie and the beauty of his bubble butt; Georgie's strong bubble butt and his beautiful blue eyes; and the $100 dollars that the tall and handsome Euro stud, Gleb Baransky, gave me just because he thought the pleasuring I gave him was the best he had ever received from anyone. I could very well imitate—while jumping from excitement, in my Ferragamo heels—HSN diva Colleen Lopez's favorite expression "Oh, oh, oh, oh, oh!"

58) The world is *my* stage. Don't fuck it up. Don't rain on my parade; or even if you make an attempt do so, make sure you take a shower first, brush your teeth and have some decent clothes on. I will not tolerate people with stinking bodies and attitude. You better be nice when you bring that face to me!

59) I may not have the *mestiza* looks that some of my cousins are so obsessed with—you know, the fair skin, aquiline nose and light brown (or blue) eyes—but one thing I have, my dear, is presence. Whenever I gracefully walk in a room with my fabulous jewelry and classy deportment, I halt conversations, turn heads and ignite curiosity. And that, my friend, is priceless. I don't need to use Facebook to *advertise* myself. I wouldn't trade my attractiveness and sexy "brown sugar" good looks for a single dose of glutathione.

60) Whenever I reach the climactic point of my orgasm I sometimes do the "Pacino scream". Do you remember that scene from The

Godfather Part III? I make no sound during the first few seconds, then I bellow like a beast afterwards.

61) I voted twice for *Dancing with the Stars* Season 13 contender Rob Kardashian; one for him and one for his big bubble butt. Bounce on me baby, bounce on me!

CHAPTER TWENTY

Final Words

Before you close the last few remaining pages of this book, I'd like to acknowledge, with deep love and respect, my mother, Elle; who gave me life, brought me into this world and taught me how to be strong and courageous amidst the chaos and craziness that surround us. Thank You, Mother Dear, for all the love, support, happiness, patience, understanding, care, concern and protection you have given me all these years. Words will never be enough to convey my message of gratitude and appreciation. To me, your accomplishments in life are at par with those of Alexander the Great, Julius Caesar, Napoleon Bonaparte, Queen Victoria and Franklin Roosevelt. You are *my* queen and warrior. You may not have conquered parts of this great big world, but in essence, you have conquered the hearts of the people who know, love and respect you. My level of respect for you is simply sky-high, and knowing you in this lifetime is one of the best things that ever happened to me. Your intelligence continues to amaze me. Your passion and determination in helping "special students" get jobs and get a better life are worthy of a thousand awards and recognitions. Yet, you do not crave for it or ask for it. You are the epitome of true grit and true class. Your smart and tactful decisions in life continue to inspire me. And the way you put bitches and jerks (especially at work) in their proper places—not with your hands, but by your stinging, straightforward words—make my own combative skills and in-your-face reproaching of imbeciles, crooks and other low life human beings seem amateurish. You fend off adversity (and assholes) with such aplomb. I truly admire you for that. The depth of my love and respect for you goes beyond infinity. Lastly, just for the heck of it, I just want to assure you that you're still the classiest and chicest of them all. I know some people try very hard to copy and emulate your sense of style, but all I can say to them is "Try again in another lifetime!" Mother Dear, you are the most beautiful mother and grandmother in the world!

To Stanley, my most dear and precious friend, thank you for taking care of me and helping me on many things. You are heaven-sent. Thank you for being my personal adviser and handyman. You are one of the smartest people I know. Your patience and perseverance amaze me especially when it comes to fixing cars and other mechanical preoccupations. Thank you also for the sweets and other desserts you serve me whenever we hang out. Even the ants are chasing me now. I thought it was only the boys who are doing it. Seriously, you are one-in-a-million and I will always cherish and appreciate the special times we've shared and continue to share. Summer 2010 will always be one of the best for me. I've seen more movies with you than my entire thirty three years of existence! You should build your own cinema! Your DVD collection is awesome. Most importantly, thank you for the good and effective advice you give me from time to time. I treasure them. Thank you also for the Ford Taurus that you gave me last Christmas and the Schwinn bicycle for my birthday! God bless you and your caring and generous heart.

To my siblings—Mikey, Mary Marie, Annie, Gracie and Erin—I don't know how long God will let me stay in this world, but in case it's time for me to say "Bye, bye," please do me a favor: take good care of Mom. Spend time with her. Take her out to lunch, dinner, the movies, the opera, the ballet and travel with her. Make time to *talk* and *listen* to her. Believe me, her advice and suggestions are very important and you will find them useful sooner or later. Be patient with her.

Also, please don't forget to guide Dillon and Princess as they grow. Instill in them the importance of education, self-respect and respect for other people regardless of their gender, sexual orientation, race and religion. This world needs more good children and people. Mold them to become good, responsible citizens of this country; a country that I love so much.

Also, remind them that we came from a respectable clan in Manila. It's very important that they know that. Instill in them the pride and good reputation that go along with our father's family name. Kids these days don't even know the names of their grandparents or great-grandparents and their family history. Having knowledge of your family history, background and lineage is very important. Our forebears in Tondo were very influential and absolutely revered, starting with our great-great grandfather, Mariano.

Lastly, take good care of yourselves. You are responsible for your own health and physical welfare, not others. You are your own guardian and protector from diseases and other unpleasant things. Eat healthy. Take your vitamins. Cut down on alcohol. Exercise! Don't miss your monthly check ups! Don't forget to relax and have your "me time"—it's good for the heart. Also, have some kind of hobby or diversion.

I treated jewelry collecting, writing, drawing, singing and dancing as hobbies and diversions, and believe me when I say that they made me very happy and feeling fulfilled and accomplished as a person. I don't need a Nobel Peace Prize award or an Oscar trophy to feel "accomplished." Screw that! I have good friends and a loving family one could ever wish for, and the feeling of contentment and satisfaction it brings surpasses all the greatest and prestigious awards combined this world has to offer.

I only have one life to live and for me, the best way to live it is by feeling satisfied and accomplished all the time. So, I hope you do the same. Life is good. Life is fun!

Do the things you really want to do, but be smart, careful and cautious as well. Before making an important decision though, think about it a thousand times.

To the good people I know who will always have my undying respect—Bobby, Mike E, Mike A, Mike W, Wade, Matt, Neal, Randy, Jason, Chris, John, Greg S, Greg J, Andrew, Alfonso, Sam, Jeff, Yuji, Maurice, Arthur, Steve R, Steve A and Don—thank you for everything. I am eternally grateful.

EPILOGUE

During the 2009 Holiday Season, I had the wonderful opportunity to be with former lovers Chris, Carl and Ronnie. Honestly, I thought I'd be permanently disabled and would need a wheelchair by New Year's Eve. These three handsome lovers possess such enormous cocks. I felt my *asspussy* had been stretched so wide that it could match the size of that meteor crater in Arizona! It was fun times for me and the boys, but certainly not for my wrecked *vajayjay*.

Chris, on the other hand, was both sexy and sentimental, with the unforgettable lines "If I weren't married I will make you my wife." Adding, "Damn baby! You're so good!"

In August 2010, his dreams came true: he filed for divorce. So, our rendezvous continues. Chris has become more handsome and mature. I love every second with him. Also, he started shaving his balls and ass crack. After a busy and stressful day, I simply find peace when I rest my face on his beautiful ass cheeks and caress that sweet spot between his balls and asshole with my sexy finger nails. His ecstatic moans are like Maria Callas and Anna Netrebko singing in my ear. Along with the sweet music comes an innate sense of validation: bitchy and nagging partners lose, and the patient, sexy, freaky bitch, Kiki Malachite, wins. Oh, such sweet taste of victory! And such sweet smelling ass!

Carl was the lover whom I have not seen for the longest time; a total of eight years. The last time we had some kind of communication was in 2002. He mentioned that he was getting married and will be moving to Tracy, CA. Last December, during our much-anticipated bedroom reunion, he mentioned he had moved from one city to another in a span of five years. Proof that life is literally a journey we have to make.

The most important thing at this point is that he is closer to where I live now. I could summon him anytime. He is such a passionate and giving lover. He was one of my most favorite boytoys back in the days. I think he still wants to be in the game.

Also, something special that came out of the 2009 Yuletide Season was the reconciliation between me and my long-time friend, Lulu. We haven't spoken in months. For some reason, we had a falling out at the start of the year. She stopped calling and I did the same thing. Maybe we were just both busy. Maybe the bitch just wanted a break from my fabulous jewelry (too blinding) and chic way of dressing (too intimidating). It could also be a tinge of jealousy. Hey, it's common among girl friends although neither one would admit it. During the ten long years that we've known each other, scenes wherein good looking men and other handsome strangers approaching me and introducing themselves—with Lulu present—have become recurring. Someone told me that "the most jealous person you could encounter is your own friend." I don't take it seriously though.

Regardless, the most important thing is that we are talking again. I couldn't really say I completely trust her these days. A person with a lot of drama and issues do not belong in my circle of friends. They belong in Dr. Phil's show! It is my prerogative though, to downgrade our level of friendship, *a`la* Standard & Poor, from friend to *frenemy*.

Not too long ago, my very first "baby boy", Russell, paid me a visit at the hotel where I regularly stay. It has been almost seven years since I last enjoyed his body and company. Russ has a bigger, muscular body and an even bigger libido these days. His lovemaking style these days is out-of-this-world. The way I used my sharp C notes during our bedroom reunion—with all my bellows and screams from the pain and pleasure—would make Pavarotti raise his prominent eyebrows with contempt. And *Mancini's Sleepworld* would promptly need to come and replace the bed that we just used.

Russ brought me to tears after he ravaged my *aching* body over and over again. They were tears of joy, absolutely. After twelve long years, my very first "baby boy" is *still* my number one lover boy.

Plus, after all, sex—good, kinky sex—should always be a fun and joyful experience.

In these times of economic mishaps and endless wars, I am still thankful. Thankful for the happiness my boys and my *bling* give me. They help me retain my sanity. I guess I'm lucky, too. And I still *get* lucky!

I simply have to live life freely with a significant amount of joy and pleasure, and no one's going to stop me from making it happen; only death. Yet, if I die tomorrow from a heart attack while having sex, I am sure I'll be embracing death with a big smile (unless, of course, the dick I am riding is so big that it really hurts; then maybe I'll die with a frown). Pick a guess!

This very moment of our lives is definitely the Age of Uncertainty. Keep that in mind, my dear friends. So, try to make the right decisions and try to do good things always. Be kind and generous to others. Don't cut people on the road because sooner or later someone might retaliate and put a bullet in your head (like what we see in the news these days). Love those who love, appreciate and respect you, but most of all, love yourself. And, of course, love the men who continue to show passion and admiration towards you. Show some appreciation, bitches! The years of "Me, me, me!" are over. There is no time to waste.

Au contraire, I really think there are only two things in life that are certain: the Beatles' legacy is forever and so is *Ob-la-di Ob-la-da*. For now, life goes on! Cheerio, darling! Cheerio!